TOTAL TRACTOR!

Written by Josephine Roberts

DK

DORLING KINDERSLEY
Senior Art Editor Jacqui Swan
Project Editor Miezan van Zyl
US Editor Margaret Parrish
Photographer Gary Ombler
DK Picture Library Claire Bowers, Rob Nunn,
Romaine Werblow
Jacket Designer Mark Cavanagh
Jacket Assistant Claire Gell
Jacket Development Manager Sophia MTT
Pre-production Producer Adam Stoneham
Producer Gemma Sharpe
Managing Editor Esther Ripley
Managing Art Editor Karen Self
Art Director Phil Ormerod
Associate Publishing Director Liz Wheeler
Publishing Director Jonathan Metcalf

DK INDIA
Senior Editor Sreshtha Bhattacharya
Senior Art Editor Chhaya Sajwan
Project Editor Suparna Sengupta
Project Art Editor Neha Sharma
Art Editor Sukriti Sobti
Assistant Editor Ira Pundeer
Assistant Art Editors Priyansha Tuli, Vansh Kohli
Managing Editor Pakshalika Jayaprakash
Managing Art Editor Arunesh Talapatra
Production Manager Pankaj Sharma
Pre-production Manager Balwant Singh
DTP Designers Vijay Kandwal, Rajesh Singh Adhikari,
Shanker Prasad
Picture Researcher Aditya Katyal
Picture Research Manager Taiyaba Khatoon

First published in the United States in 2015 by
DK Publishing, 345 Hudson Street,
New York, New York 10014

A Penguin Random House Company

CONTENTS

01 POWERFUL MACHINES

02 ON THE FARM

03 BEYOND THE FIELDS

INTRODUCTION

Welcome to the amazing, diverse world of Tractors! For more than a century, tractors have steadily evolved to suit our needs, and as our engineering skills have improved we have moved from creating simple engines on steel wheels, to the complex, specialized machines of today.

We depend on tractors of all shapes and sizes to produce our food and materials, and to maintain our parks and roads, but tractors can be fun too. In this book we have cool tractors, cute tractors, and crazy-looking tractors—drive on in, and see if you can find your favorites.

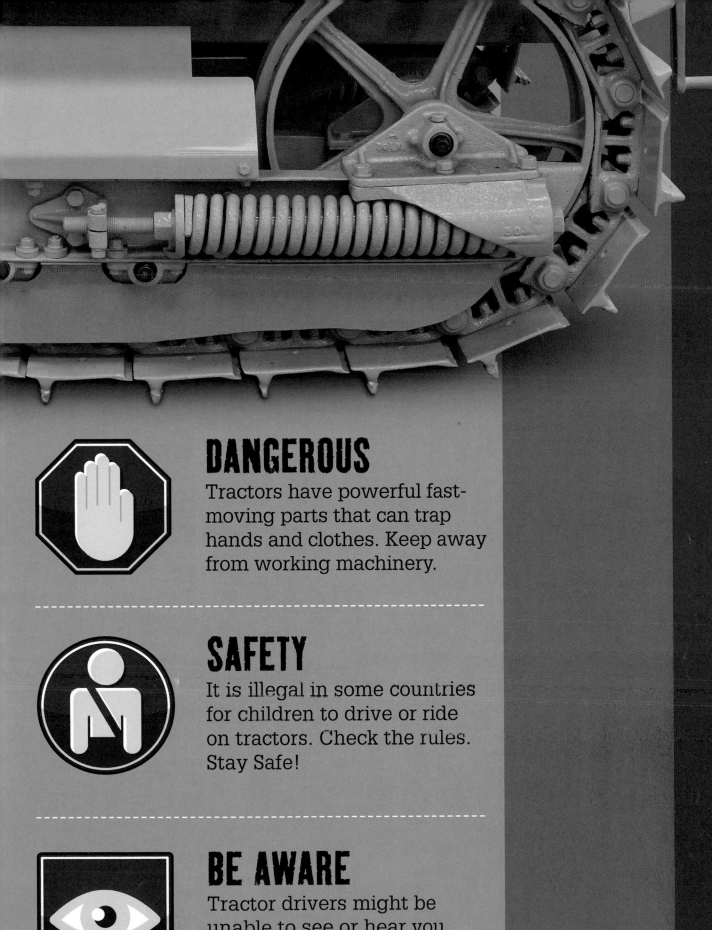

DANGEROUS

Tractors have powerful fast-moving parts that can trap hands and clothes. Keep away from working machinery.

SAFETY

It is illegal in some countries for children to drive or ride on tractors. Check the rules. Stay Safe!

BE AWARE

Tractor drivers might be unable to see or hear you, so you must steer clear of tractors on the move.

POWERFUL MACHINES

01

MODERN TRACTOR

Today's tractors are powerful machines that can tow massive weights over rough terrain and power a vast range of machinery. The strength of a tractor's engine is usually given in horsepower (hp)—a term dating back to when steam engines were designed to replace working horses.

" **Massey Ferguson tractors are easy to spot, since they are almost always red with gray wheels.** "

Grille

Weight frame for attaching weights

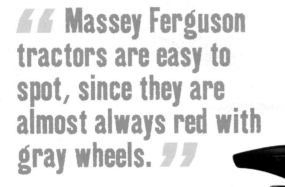

MASSEY FER

Tires are 122 in (310 cm) wide

READY TO ROLL ON

Tractors are built in many different countries. The new tractors are transported by truck, train, or ship, and they are sent to dealers worldwide who sell them to farmers. These large tractors are ready to be driven on to a ship, but smaller ones are sometimes shipped in parts and then assembled when they reach their destination.

STEAM POWER

Before tractors were invented we relied on steam engines for powering farm machinery and towing heavy loads. Steam engines remained popular until they were replaced by more efficient internal combustion engines—engines that work the same way as those you find in cars today.

This steam-driven tractor has a coal fire in its firebox. This heats water in the boiler to create steam. Under high pressure, the steam drives the mechanical parts that turn the driving wheels to move the tractor forward.

SPEED
Its top speed is about 5 mph (8 km/h).

Safety valve

Funnel

Regulator

Piston

Smokebox

Iron wheel

Boiler

Steering chain turns front wheel

DORO

SEAWAYS

" Clayton & Shuttleworth did not just make machines for farmers—it also made airplanes. "

13 ft (4 m)

23 ft (7 m)

CLAYTON & SHUTTLEWORTH DOROTHY

ORIGIN UK
FIRST PRODUCED 1914
WEIGHT 22,000 lb (10,000 kg)
POWER 5 hp

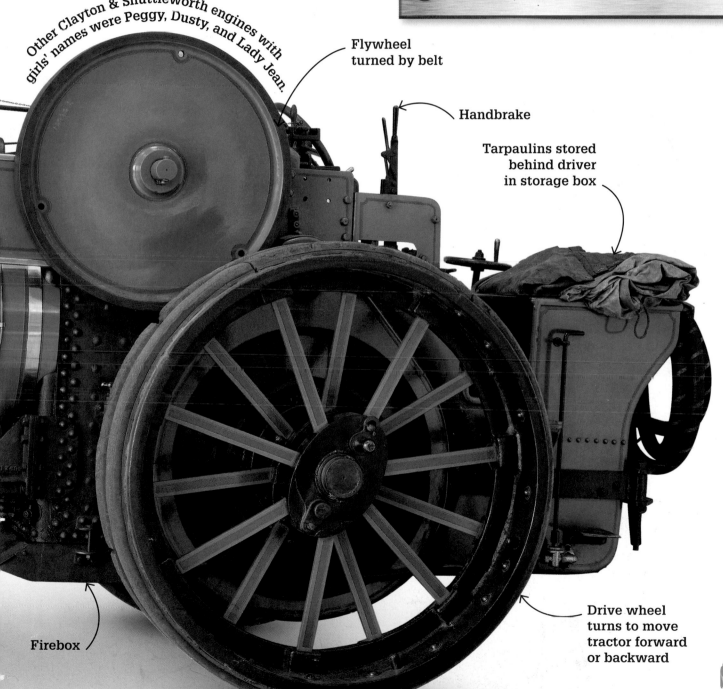

Other Clayton & Shuttleworth engines with girls' names were Peggy, Dusty, and Lady Jean.

Flywheel turned by belt

Handbrake

Tarpaulins stored behind driver in storage box

Firebox

Drive wheel turns to move tractor forward or backward

STEAM ENGINES

Most steam tractors were incredibly strong when it came to powering or pulling heavy farm machinery, but they moved very slowly. These hulking engines weren't always faster than the horses they were replacing, but they were certainly stronger.

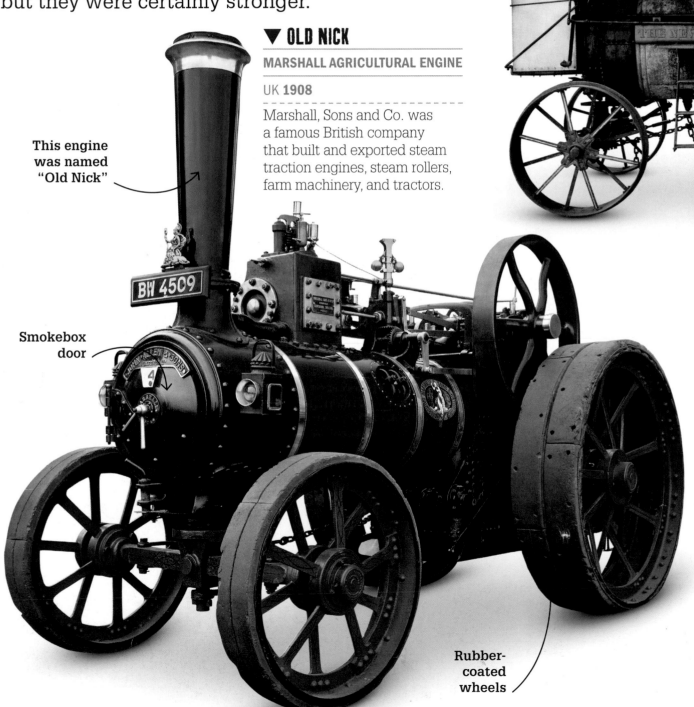

▼ OLD NICK

MARSHALL AGRICULTURAL ENGINE

UK **1908**

Marshall, Sons and Co. was a famous British company that built and exported steam traction engines, steam rollers, farm machinery, and tractors.

This engine was named "Old Nick"

BW 4509

Smokebox door

Rubber-coated wheels

◀ PRAIRIE STEAMER

HUBER NO.185 | **USA 1915**

This was one of the first prairie tractors, designed to help farmers turn America's vast fields into productive farmland.

Protective shelter for driver and engine

▼ PLOW MASTER

FOWLER PLOWING ENGINE AA7

UK 1917

These machines worked in pairs. Parked up, they would winch a huge plow from one side of the field to the other.

Winch drum

Steam dome

▶ UNUSUAL DESIGN

AVERY | **UK 1911**

This highly unusual 40-horsepower tractor, with its engine mounted underneath, looked more like a railroad locomotive.

Under-mounted engine

Boiler

◀ LAST DAYS OF STEAM

BRYAN LIGHT STEAM TRACTOR

USA c.1920

The water in this machine was heated using kerosene instead of coal, which made it possible to heat much faster.

FACT
The boiler on a steam tractor had to be tested regularly to make sure that it wouldn't blow up.

17

FIRST TRACTORS

British inventor Daniel Albone (to the right in this picture) was already famous for racing and making bicycles when he invented the first successful lightweight tractor. In 1902, Albone created his "Ivel Agricultural Motor," which won many awards. Only around 500 of these tractors were ever made.

EARLY TRACTORS

By the beginning of the 20th century, steam power was a thing of the past. Manufacturers began to produce gas-powered tractors, hoping to convince the modern farmer to stop using horses for farm work, and to buy one of their marvelous new machines.

Belt and pulley to power farm machinery

▲ ONE OF THE FIRST

IVEL AGRICULTURAL MOTOR | UK **1902**

This lightweight gas-powered tractor had one forward and one reverse gear, and it was capable of producing 8 horsepower.

A canopy on top keeps the sun off the driver's head.

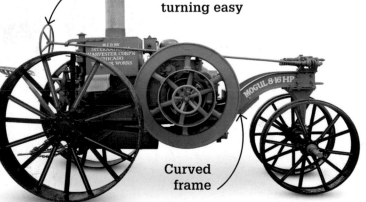

USES KEROSENE ALL LOADS

◀ ORIGINAL TRACTORS

HART-PARR 20–40 | USA **1920**

These giant tractors were built in Iowa and were made for farming the huge, flat prairie lands.

Hart-Parr was the first company to advertise their engines as "tractors"

Improved steering system made turning easy

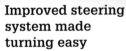

Curved frame

◀ BEST SELLER

INTERNATIONAL HARVESTER MOGUL

USA **1914**

Built in the US, "Mogul" tractors proved very popular. They were shipped all over the world to many countries.

Powered by kerosene, the fuel tank sits at the front of the tractor.

▶ HEAVYWEIGHT

RUMELY OIL PULL

USA **1910**

These tractors, made by the Advance-Rumely Company, were large, heavy machines. They were powered by kerosene and cooled by oil.

Wide rear wheels

FACT

The first Oil Pull was known as Kerosene Annie.

Engine kept cool by water

◀ WATER-COOLED ENGINE

| INTERNATIONAL HARVESTER TITAN | USA **1917** |

By the time the International Harvester Company built the "Titan," it had become the world's leading tractor manufacturer.

▼ STAR PERFORMER

WATERLOO BOY

USA **1917**

The Waterloo Gasoline Engine Company was bought by John Deere, and its tractors formed the basis for John Deere's first tractors.

Mid-mounted radiator

WATERLOO BOY

Steel lugs on wheels give extra grip on soft ground

21

CHANGING SHAPE

As technology improved, tractors became smaller, lighter, and easier to use. They looked more like modern tractors in shape. The new machines were more affordable, so most farmers could buy their own tractor. Using tractors instead of horses meant farmers could farm more land with fewer workers.

20 hp, 4-cylinder engine

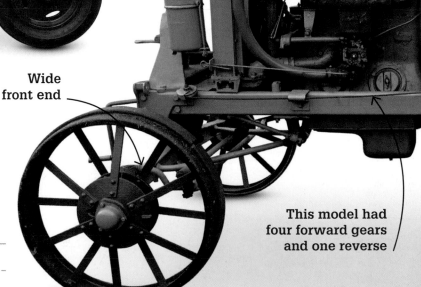

▲ TRACTOR FOR THE MASSES

FORDSON MODEL F	USA **1917**

The Fordson Model F was said to be the first small, lightweight, mass-produced, and affordable tractor in the world.

Wide mudguard

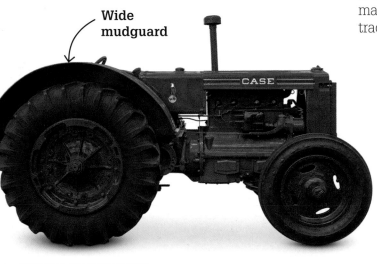

Steering column

Wide front end

This model had four forward gears and one reverse

▲ POWER PERFORMER

CASE MODEL C	USA **1929**

This eye-catching little tractor had a modern streamlined appearance. It was powered by a four-cylinder gas engine.

▶ ALL-PURPOSE TRACTOR

FARMALL F-20	USA **1932**

This lightweight, easy-to-steer tractor was perfect for working in crop fields. It was also available in tricycle format.

◀ **SETTING THE STANDARD**

| FORD 9N | USA **1939** |

The first tractor to be given the Ford name was the 9N. This simple and easy-to-use tractor featured a three-point hitch and a rear power takeoff shaft to power attached implements.

Exhaust fit underneath, just like a car

Cowling protects driver's hand and feet from wind and rain

Some early David Brown tractors had double seats

▶ **MORE SPEED, MORE STYLE**

| DAVID BROWN VAK 1 | UK **1939** |

This tractor had a unique rounded design, plus a cowling around the dashboard to keep the driver warm in the cold British winters.

Between 1932 and 1939, 148,690 of these tractors were made.

Steel wheels

Rubber tires

▲ **LITTLE GREY FERGIE**

| FERGUSON TE-20 | UK **1946** |

This world-famous tractor was designed and built by Irish engineer and inventor Harry Ferguson, and it is still popular with collectors today.

23

TRICYCLE TRACTOR

Tricycle, or narrow front-end tractors as they are sometimes called, were specially designed to work between rows of planted crops. These lightweight tractors could tread carefully between crops, were extremely easy to steer, and could pivot around in a small circle. This made them ideal for working in confined spaces.

Today, tricycle tractors look unusual, but in the US and Canada in the 1930s–50s, the tricycle was the most commonplace tractor design.

A range of implements (tools) could be used with the tricycle tractor. Here, a "ridger" is being pulled through the plowed land, to make neat rows for the seed to be sowed in.

Radiator cap

Fuel cap

Air cleaner filters air before it enters engine

The Ge

Starting handle

Single front wheel

FACT

Tricycle tractors are unstable on bumpy ground and can sometimes roll over.

4.5ft (1.4m)

9.8ft (3m)

CLETRAC GENERAL

ORIGIN USA
FIRST PRODUCED 1939
WEIGHT 3,110lb (1,410kg)
POWER 17hp

Some people have even used tricycle tractors in "dancing tractor" displays.

High clearance frame allows tractor to drive over crops without damaging them

Adjustable-width rear wheels

25

SWITCHING TO DIESEL

Diesel engines have many advantages over gas engines—diesel is more efficient than gas, it is safer, because it won't blow up, and the engines tend to be more durable. Despite these advantages, diesel-powered tractors were not common until the 1960s.

4-cylinder diesel engine

Steel tracks

▲ TRACKED POWER

CATERPILLAR SIXTY | USA **1931**

The first diesel Caterpillar did not sell very well because farmers weren't used to diesel. Eventually, however, it became the fuel of choice for all modern farmers.

▶ DIESEL DOWN UNDER

McDONALD TWB | AUSTRALIA **1932**

This Australian "hot bulb" diesel tractor was designed by the pioneering McDonald Brothers of Melbourne. The popular TWB was based on both the Lanz Bulldog and Rumely tractors.

Fan to cool engine

Large muffler

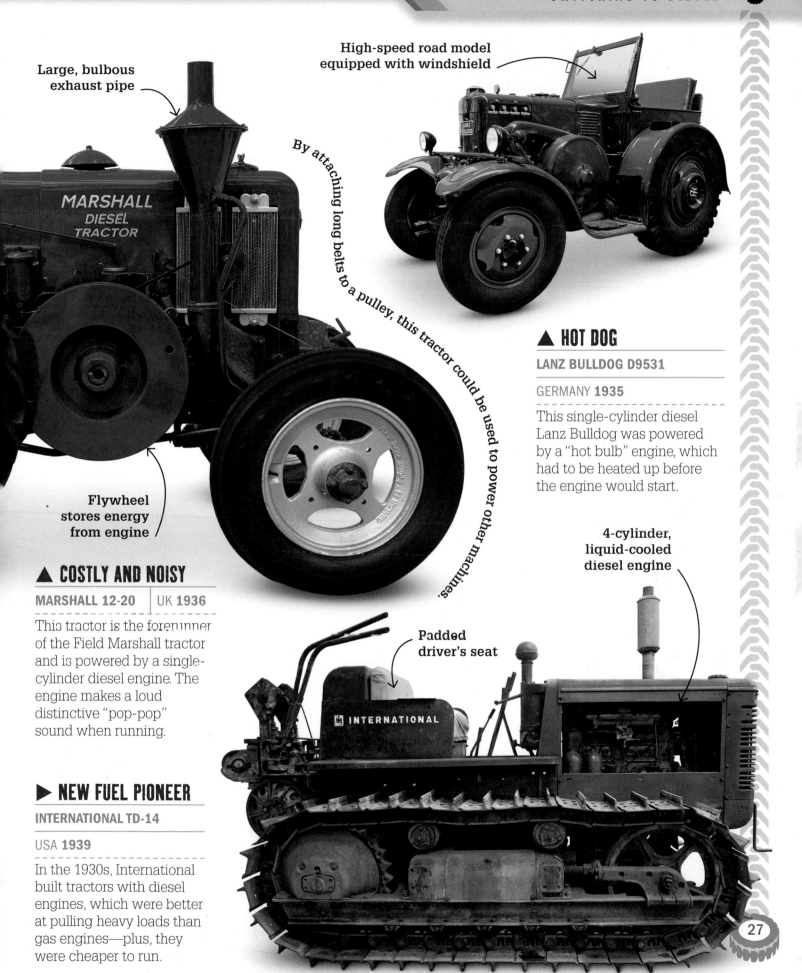

Large, bulbous
exhaust pipe

High-speed road model
equipped with windshield

MARSHALL
DIESEL
TRACTOR

By attaching long belts to a pulley, this tractor could be used to power other machines.

Flywheel
stores energy
from engine

▲ HOT DOG

LANZ BULLDOG D9531

GERMANY **1935**

This single-cylinder diesel
Lanz Bulldog was powered
by a "hot bulb" engine, which
had to be heated up before
the engine would start.

▲ COSTLY AND NOISY

MARSHALL 12-20 | UK **1936**

This tractor is the forerunner
of the Field Marshall tractor
and is powered by a single-
cylinder diesel engine. The
engine makes a loud
distinctive "pop-pop"
sound when running.

4-cylinder,
liquid-cooled
diesel engine

Padded
driver's seat

IH INTERNATIONAL

▶ NEW FUEL PIONEER

INTERNATIONAL TD-14

USA **1939**

In the 1930s, International
built tractors with diesel
engines, which were better
at pulling heavy loads than
gas engines—plus, they
were cheaper to run.

9½ ft (2.9 m)

16 ft (4.9 m)

NEW HOLLAND T6.140 METHANE POWER

ORIGIN USA
FIRST PRODUCED 2013 (prototype)
WEIGHT 20,000 lb (9,000 kg)
POWER 135 hp

FACT
Methane tractors produce 80 percent less harmful emissions than diesel tractors.

Comfortable safety cab

NEW

ALTERNATIVE FUEL SOURCES

Most tractors use huge amounts of diesel, an expensive, nonrenewable fossil fuel. Scientists are working to produce other fuels that are more sustainable and less harmful to the environment, such as methane gas (from animal manure) and biofuels (from fermented crops).

SUSTAINABLE FARMING

If a farm can produce its own fuel it can save money and help the environment. Sustainable farms can use animals or crops to produce their own fuel. Animal manure gives off methane gas, and crops such as sunflowers, oilseed rape, and sugar cane can be fermented to produce biofuels.

Methane is produced from manure, or biofuels are made from fermented crops

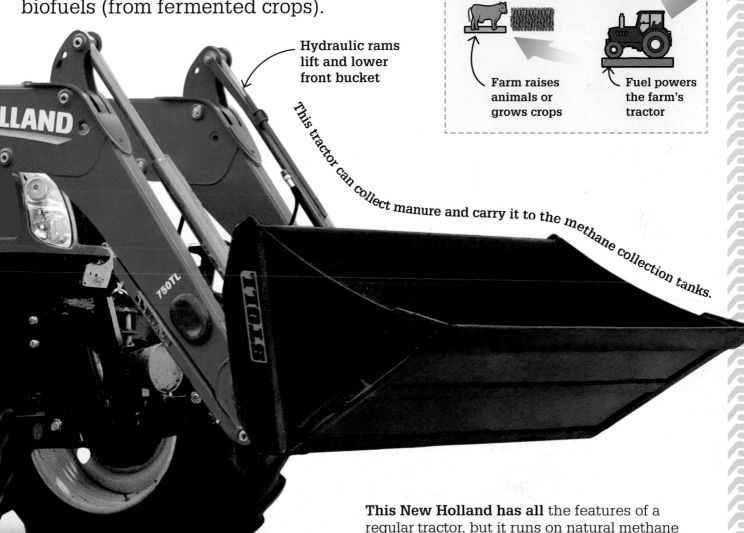

Farm raises animals or grows crops

Fuel powers the farm's tractor

Hydraulic rams lift and lower front bucket

This tractor can collect manure and carry it to the methane collection tanks.

OLLAND

750TL

STOLL

This New Holland has all the features of a regular tractor, but it runs on natural methane gas instead of diesel. Methane produces fewer pollutants, and a methane-powered engine runs more quietly than one powered by diesel.

FUTURE FARMING

Tractors have to adapt to suit changing needs. As populations grow, more efficient machines are needed to help produce enough food and materials. Valtra's ANTS concept tractor exists only as a model, but it could shape the future of tractor design. It is a versatile machine that can be adapted to any task.

TIRES AND TREADS

Tractors are versatile and can work on many different types of terrain, but some surfaces demand specialized wheels or tires. Most tractor wheels and tires can be removed and changed when necessary. Various tire tread patterns are used for different kinds of work.

DEALING WITH WINTER

Snow and ice can be extremely slippery, and chunky rubber tires don't always provide enough grip for such conditions. One way to gain extra traction is to cover the wheels in tire chains. The chain links cut into the packed snow and allow the tractor to move along safely.

In the past, most tractor wheels were made of steel. Extra grip was provided by pointed teeth (spade lugs) on the rim of the wheel.

Spade lugs provide extra grip when working in soil

Plain steel front wheel

Removable road band prevents damage to roads or fields

SPADE LUGS

ROAD BANDS

This Massey Harris had four-wheel drive.

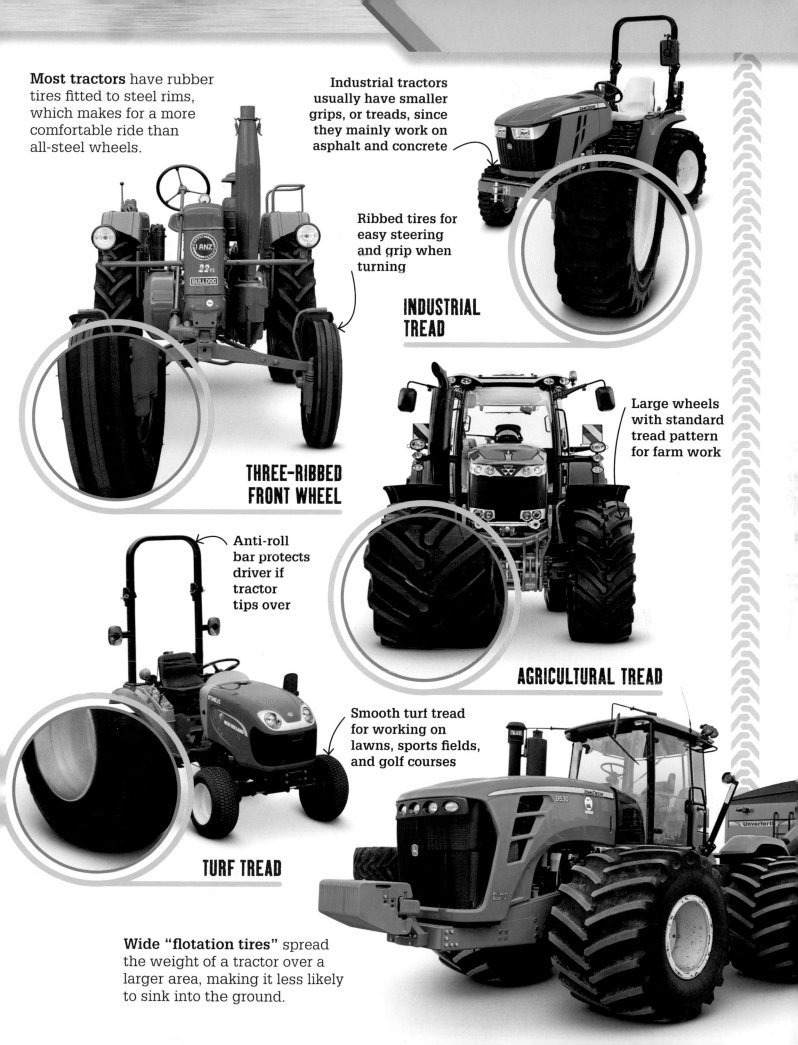

Most tractors have rubber tires fitted to steel rims, which makes for a more comfortable ride than all-steel wheels.

Industrial tractors usually have smaller grips, or treads, since they mainly work on asphalt and concrete

Ribbed tires for easy steering and grip when turning

INDUSTRIAL TREAD

THREE-RIBBED FRONT WHEEL

Large wheels with standard tread pattern for farm work

Anti-roll bar protects driver if tractor tips over

AGRICULTURAL TREAD

Smooth turf tread for working on lawns, sports fields, and golf courses

TURF TREAD

Wide "flotation tires" spread the weight of a tractor over a larger area, making it less likely to sink into the ground.

TO THE SOUTH POLE

These reliable Ferguson tractors carried the explorer Sir Edmund Hillary (left) and his crew to the South Pole in 1958. The "Fergies" were equipped with an extra wheel on each side and caterpillar tracks, to provide grip in the snow and ice. Canvas cabs helped to give the drivers some protection from the bitter cold.

CRAWLERS

Crawler tractors move on tracks instead of wheels, and are great for working on uneven ground, mud, and snow. The tracks spread the crawler's weight evenly over the ground and provide these all-terrain vehicles with excellent grip and stability.

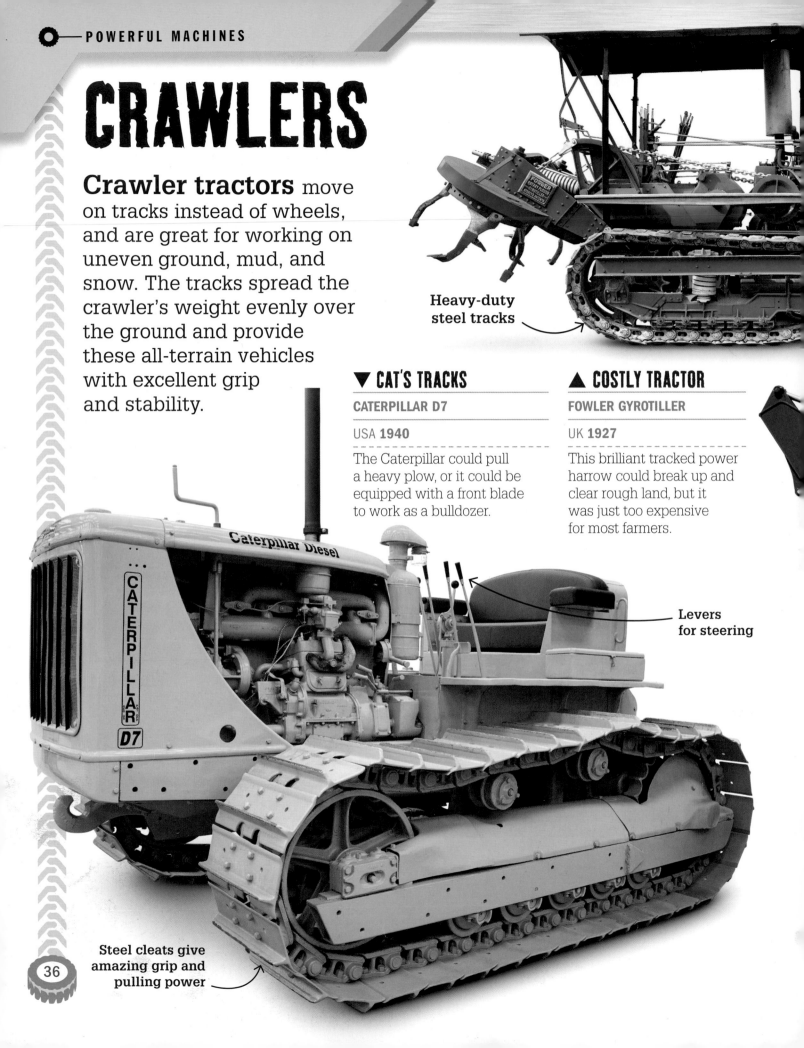

Heavy-duty steel tracks

▼ CAT'S TRACKS

CATERPILLAR D7

USA 1940

The Caterpillar could pull a heavy plow, or it could be equipped with a front blade to work as a bulldozer.

▲ COSTLY TRACTOR

FOWLER GYROTILLER

UK 1927

This brilliant tracked power harrow could break up and clear rough land, but it was just too expensive for most farmers.

Levers for steering

Steel cleats give amazing grip and pulling power

HOW A CRAWLER WORKS

The drive sprocket has teeth that lock into the slots on the inside of the track and pull it around, working in the same way as a bicycle chain. The idler wheel and the rollers hold the track in place as it moves around the track frame.

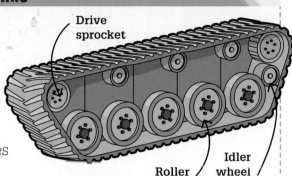

Drive sprocket

Roller

Idler wheel

Drive sprocket

This digger can swivel all around while the tracks remain still.

Small cleats

Track frame

▲ TANK TRACKS

ALVIS FV103 SPARTAN	UK 1978

These armored personnel carriers have served the British Army for decades, and they can travel at up to 60 mph (95 km/h).

◄ DIRT DIGGER

JOHN DEERE 160D LC	USA 2007

Tracked diggers like this help to build roads. Sharp stones on construction sites can puncture tires, but tracks are super tough and resilient.

► TURNING TO RUBBER

JOHN DEERE 333E TRACK LOADER

USA 2013

This loader has a triangular drive track system and rubber tracks, which are ideal for working on tarmac and concrete since they don't damage the surface.

37

RUBBER TRACKS

Tracked tractors, or crawlers, are slower than wheeled tractors, but they have an advantage when the going gets sticky. The tracks spread the weight of the tractor over a much larger area, preventing it from slipping or getting stuck in soft surfaces, such as muddy ground, sand, and snow.

" Challenger was the first manufacturer to produce a rubber-tracked farm tractor nearly 30 years ago. "

Exhaust expels fumes from diesel engine

Side mirror

Headlight

Weights help to balance tractor when pulling a heavy load

Challenger introduced rubber tracks to allow tracked farm tractors to also drive on roads. The metal tracks of early crawlers sometimes ripped up paved surfaces.

Sturdy rubber track

MT 765D

12 ft (3.4 m)

20 ft (6 m)

CHALLENGER MT765D

ORIGIN USA
FIRST PRODUCED 2012
WEIGHT 31,075 lb (14,095 kg)
POWER 350 hp

Safety cab

Indicator lights are used when driving on roads

Drive wheels

Rear linkage

SPEEDING UP

Most agricultural work is slow and steady, but many tractors also have to travel on the roads—from the farm to the market, for instance. These tractors are designed for tasks where speed really does matter.

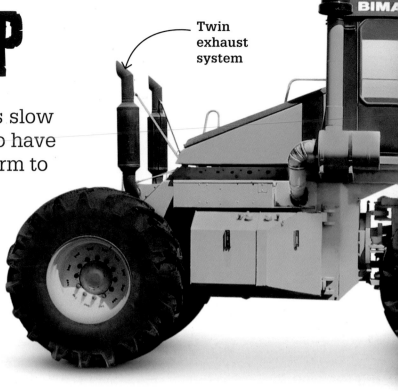

Twin exhaust system

▲ PACY PERFORMER

BIMA 360	FRANCE **1983**

This high-powered Bima 360 was built in Velye, France, and features both front and rear power takeoff, and linkage. It has a unique front-mounted cab, which gives the driver excellent visibility.

Fuel-efficient engine

High cab

▲ BUILT FOR SPEED

TRANTOR MK II	UK **1983**

This high-speed transport tractor was way ahead of its time, being one of the first machines designed to do the work of both a tractor and a truck.

▶ SPEEDING UP

MB TRAC 1000

GERMANY **1980**

Compared to the other tractors of the early 1980s, the MB Trac, made by Mercedes Benz, was extremely fast and futuristic.

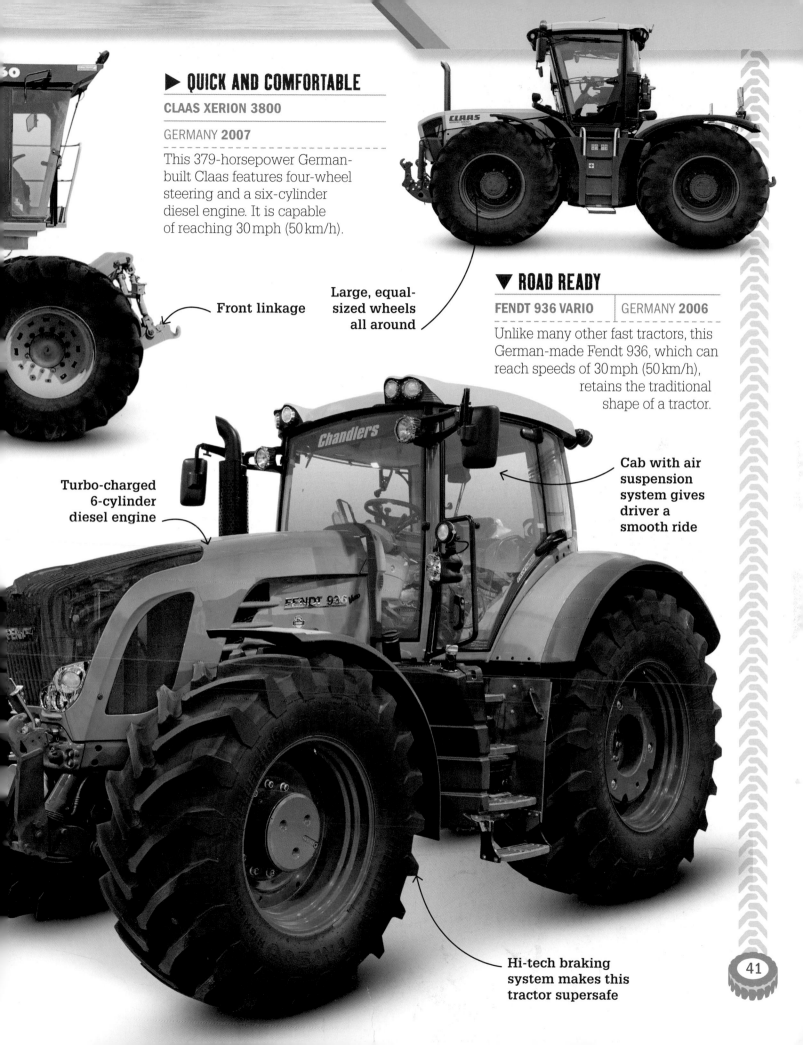

▶ QUICK AND COMFORTABLE

CLAAS XERION 3800

GERMANY **2007**

This 379-horsepower German-built Claas features four-wheel steering and a six-cylinder diesel engine. It is capable of reaching 30 mph (50 km/h).

Front linkage

Large, equal-sized wheels all around

▼ ROAD READY

| **FENDT 936 VARIO** | GERMANY **2006** |

Unlike many other fast tractors, this German-made Fendt 936, which can reach speeds of 30 mph (50 km/h), retains the traditional shape of a tractor.

Cab with air suspension system gives driver a smooth ride

Turbo-charged 6-cylinder diesel engine

Hi-tech braking system makes this tractor supersafe

SPEEDSTER

The amazing JCB Fastrac was designed not only for strength, but also for speed. These super-fast tractors can be used for everyday farm work, but they can also travel quickly and comfortably on the roads, making them perfect for towing heavy loads at high speeds.

Many farm tractors can be bouncy and uncomfortable when driven at their top speed, but the JCB Fastrac has a unique all-around suspension system. This provides the driver with a safe, smooth ride.

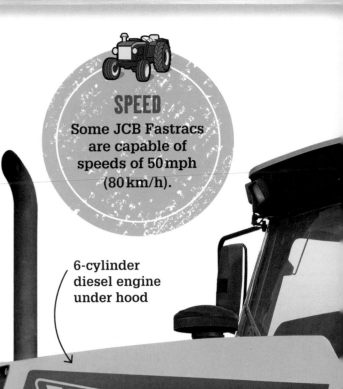

SPEED
Some JCB Fastracs are capable of speeds of 50 mph (80 km/h).

6-cylinder diesel engine under hood

Hydraulic arms for lifting and lowering farm implements

Large, equal-sized wheels

The spacious, centrally mounted cab gives the driver a smooth, balanced ride.

10ft (3m)

18.4ft (5.8m)

JCB FASTRAC 185-65

ORIGIN UK
FIRST PRODUCED 1994
WEIGHT 14,300lb (6,500kg)
POWER 188hp

Top link attaches
farm implement
to tractor

Rear
mudguard

SELECTRONIC

JCB

Steps to
the cab

TRACTOR CABS

Early tractors had no cabs, and so the driver had to brave the weather conditions and risked injury if the tractor rolled over. These tractors were also noisy and tiring to drive. Today's machines have comfortable seats in quiet safety cabs packed with buttons, joysticks, and computer monitors.

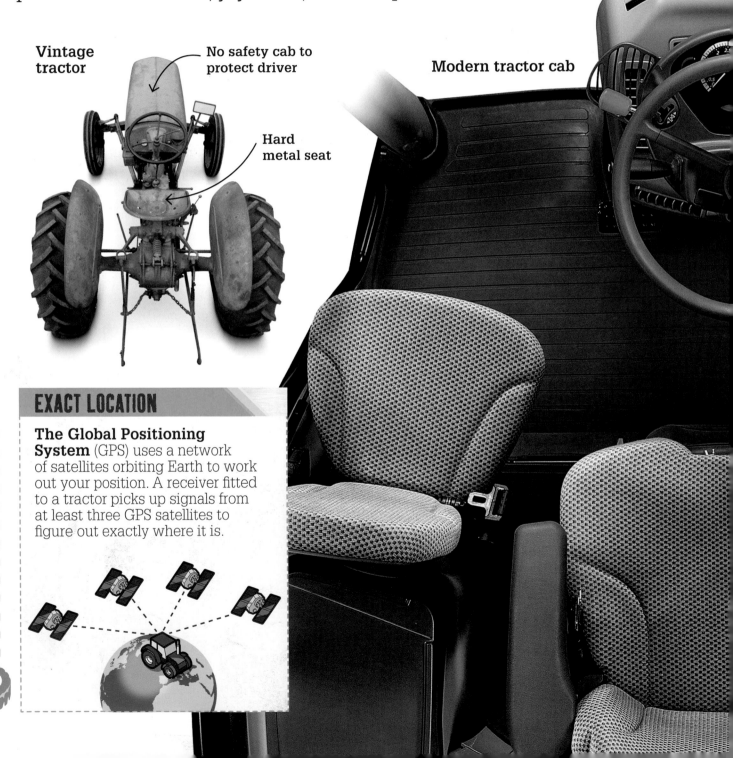

Vintage tractor

No safety cab to protect driver

Hard metal seat

Modern tractor cab

EXACT LOCATION

The Global Positioning System (GPS) uses a network of satellites orbiting Earth to work out your position. A receiver fitted to a tractor picks up signals from at least three GPS satellites to figure out exactly where it is.

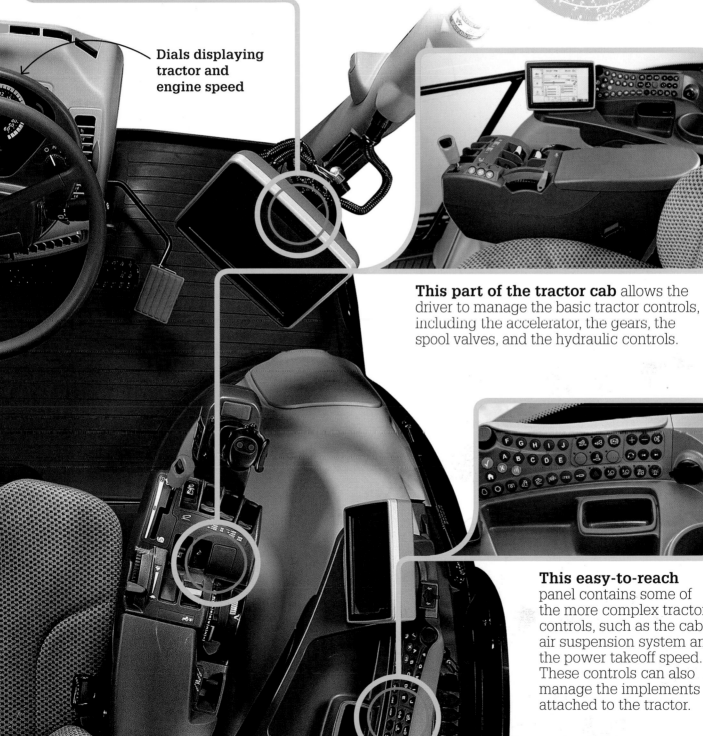

Satellite navigation (GPS) helps the farmer to calculate the exact area of a field, which assists with the even distribution of seeds, fertilizers, or pesticides.

FACT

The first cabs made for tractors were simple weatherproof covers.

Dials displaying tractor and engine speed

This part of the tractor cab allows the driver to manage the basic tractor controls, including the accelerator, the gears, the spool valves, and the hydraulic controls.

This easy-to-reach panel contains some of the more complex tractor controls, such as the cab's air suspension system and the power takeoff speed. These controls can also manage the implements attached to the tractor.

ENGINES AT PLAY

Tractors are hardworking

machines—but they can be lots of fun too. Huge numbers of people of all ages enjoy attending agricultural fairs and vintage shows. These events are great places to see all kinds of tractors, learn more about your favorites, and spot machines you've never seen before.

Safety cab protects driver

Hydraulic ram to control bucket

A display team of JCB Backhoe Loaders, known as the "Dancing Diggers," wows the crowds.

Dancing Farmalls entertain the crowds with a choreographed dance, which takes a lot of skill and precision to perform.

Tractor road runs are exciting. Drivers (and tractors) sometimes wear costumes, and the goal is to raise money for charity.

Hydraulic ram to control lifting arm

The highly skilled drivers use these JCB Backhoe Loaders to perform stunts at crazy angles.

Vintage fairs and shows
feature collectable antique tractors, and owners are usually happy to answer questions about their tractors.

Tractor plowing
is an international sport. Drivers compete in specialty classes to see who can produce the neatest furrows.

"Brek 't o

Castrol

CP
CARRILLO

CLAAS

THE PULLING GAME

This highly modified tractor is taking part in the world's most powerful motorsport— power pulling. Automobile enthusiasts and engineers create these crazy-looking, supercharged tractors, some of which even have jet engines! Drivers compete to see which tractor can tow a huge sledge the farthest, over a 330-ft (100-m) track.

TRACTOR RESTORATION

Vintage and classic tractors are hugely collectable, and many people enjoy restoring and preserving these fascinating old machines. Damaged mechanical parts are repaired or replaced and the tractor is repainted—giving an old wreck a whole new lease of life.

STILL WORKING

Some collectors prefer to let their tractors age naturally. The David Brown 25 below dates from 1953, and has never been restored. The original red paint has faded with time, but the tractor is mechanically well maintained, and remains in good working order. These unpainted "original" tractors can be preserved by applying oil or lacquer to the tinwork.

Before restoration, this Farmall H had worn paintwork and tires, and definitely needed a new exhaust pipe.

After restoration, Riley Hanson's tractor looks just like it did when it was brand new in 1953.

Tractor has been repainted in its original colors

451 CUBES

case 1070

Ryan Haass and his Case 1070 tractor won the grand prize at the 2012 Delo Tractor Restoration Competition, based in the US.

This old Case tractor has cracked tires and plenty of dirt and rust—making it an ideal candidate for a restoration project.

New stickers, or decals, have to be carefully reapplied

Restorers often buy new tires, since the old ones may be worn and cracked

This 1966 John Deere high-crop tractor had suffered a lot of wear and tear, and the paintwork was faded.

A team of restorers from Decatur, Texas, had to work hard to produce this pristine award-winning restoration job.

TOY TRACTORS

People of all ages are fascinated by the scaled-down world of tiny tractors. Most of these miniature tractors are fun toys, but some of the older models can be rare, collectable, and valuable.

▲ **OVER THE TOP** | 1920s

This fun clockwork tractor was made in New York. When wound, it can climb over obstacles.

◀ **WIND-UP TRACTOR** | 1960s

A tiny key winds this farm tractor up, and the clockwork mechanism powers it along. It can tow many attachments, including this disk harrow.

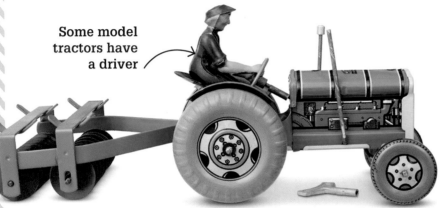

Some model tractors have a driver

▶ **REVERSIBLE MECHANISM** | 1967

This model of a 1940s Zetor tractor is powered by clockwork, so it needs to be wound up. Amazingly, it has three forward gears and a reverse gear.

Painted grille bars

"MATCHBOX" Series
72 72
A LESNEY PRODUCT

▲ **TINY DIE-CAST TRACTOR** | 1959

Many companies make tiny scale models of their tractors, such as this matchbox-sized Fordson Major.

▶ **SPRING-COILED** | 1916

This toy tractor has a spring inside, so it speeds forward when pulled back and released.

Older toys were often made from tin

Miniature tow rope to pull along

▲ EDUCATIONAL TOY | 1950–60

This colorful plastic tractor can be taken apart to show how a real tractor is put together.

Driver's arms and legs move

▲ MIGHTY BULL | 1960s

This detailed little tin-plate tractor was made in Japan. It has a vibrating engine and moves along on tracks just like a real crawler tractor.

▲ TRICKY TOMMY | 1960s

This vintage, battery-powered toy tractor has a plastic body, tin-plate back wheels, and a driver.

Rubber front wheels

RIDE-ON TRACTORS

Driving a toy tractor is lots of fun. Some ride-on toys are pedal-powered, but others run on battery and even have a brake and accelerator, just like the real thing. These tractors may be small, but it is important always to wear a helmet, especially if speeding along on hard surfaces.

▲ WIND-UP CRAWLER | 1960s

This German-built, tin-plate, wind-up tractor is a fascinating toy—it shows exactly how crawler tracks really work.

Wheels drive along the inside of beltlike tracks

ON THE FARM

02

TRACTORS AROUND THE WORLD

Tractors are manufactured in many different countries, and some of the lesser-known companies often produce the most affordable machines. Huge numbers of popular, compact tractors are made in China and India.

Sloping hood

RENAULT

Ares 710 RZ

▶ INTERNATIONAL TRACTOR

BELARUS 952

REPUBLIC OF BELARUS **1995**

The Minsk Tractor Works in Belarus produces about eight percent of the world's wheeled tractors. They are considered reliable, simple, and affordable.

▲ FRENCH FLAIR

RENAULT ARES 710 RZ | FRANCE **2009**

Some manufacturers use tractor parts made by other companies. This tractor is equipped with a six-cylinder John Deere engine.

▼ RELIABLE ALL-AROUNDER

SONALIKA SOLIS-20 | INDIA **2010**

These low-cost, compact, Indian-made tractors are popular with hobby farmers and small-scale farmers. This model has a three-cylinder, 18.5-horsepower Mitsubishi engine.

Front weights

Small, lightweight implements

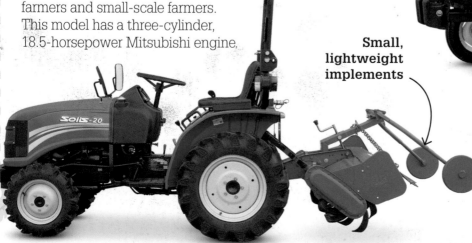

▲ AFFORDABLE PERFORMER

YTO 180 | CHINA **2014**

Some of the world's most inexpensive tractors are made in China. This 18-horsepower YTO tractor is ideal for small businesses.

Rear mudguard

▶ COMPACT 4X4

KUBOTA L3200 | JAPAN **2012**

This mini four-wheel-drive tractor has a 31-horsepower engine; it can be equipped with a front bucket and backhoe loader.

Foldable roll bar

▶ POWERFUL PACKAGE

ZETOR MAJOR 80

CZECH REPUBLIC **2013**

Zetor produces straightforward, reliable tractors. This is a four-wheel-drive model fitted with an 80-horsepower engine.

Exhaust pipe

Fuel tank situated beside the steps to driver's cab

LAND GIRLS

During World War II, there was a huge shortage of farm workers because so many British men were serving as soldiers. Hired by the government, "Land Girls" came to the rescue by learning how to drive tractors, plow fields, and harvest crops. This Land Girl is using a Fordson Model N tractor.

POWER POINTS

Early tractors were used simply to replace the pulling power of the working horse, but today's tractors are much more complex machines. Their mighty engines can be used to power a wide range of tools and equipment.

ENERGY
The engine's power is turned into electricity by a generator called an alternator.

This close-up image shows a power socket (to the right) and an air-brake socket (to the left). These are used to connect a trailer to the tractor, to power the lights, and to ensure that the trailer brakes at the same time as the tractor.

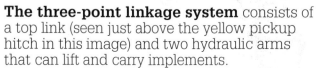

The three-point linkage system consists of a top link (seen just above the yellow pickup hitch in this image) and two hydraulic arms that can lift and carry implements.

Hydraulic pipes (filled with liquid) are plugged into these sockets to operate the rams that lift and tip loaders and trailers.

The power takeoff (PTO) shaft is a rotating rod that takes power from the engine to drive equipment such as balers. It spins at high speed and can be very dangerous.

The pickup hitch is a hook that enables the tractor driver to lift and attach trailers and implements without having to leave the cab.

PRAIRIE GIANT

The wide-open prairies of North America required massive tractors to break up the soil. These large, heavy tractors used huge amounts of fuel, and they were so tall that operators had to climb a flight of steps just to reach the engine.

The prairies were vast grassland that hadn't been farmed on a mass scale. Twin City tractors helped American farmers turn the untamed wilderness into productive farmland.

Roof protects engine from sun and rain

Front cowling covers engine

Solid iron wheels

Steering connects to front wheels

Kerosene engine

10 ft (3.1 m)
20 ft (6 m)

TWIN CITY 40-65

ORIGIN USA
FIRST PRODUCED 1916
WEIGHT 23,700 lb (10,750 kg)
POWER Drawbar 40 hp; Belt 65 hp

The driver steps up on to the back to drive this tractor.

Steps to
reach engine

Rear wheels are like
those on a steam-
traction engine

TWO-IN-ONE

Probably the weirdest tractor transformation of all is the Doe Triple-D. The first double tractor was built by British farmer George Pryor. He then enlisted Ernest Doe & Sons to improve on his crazy-looking idea, which it did by joining two Fordson Major tractors together.

FACT

When traveling on the road, a Doe Triple-D tractor can be driven with just one engine running, to save fuel.

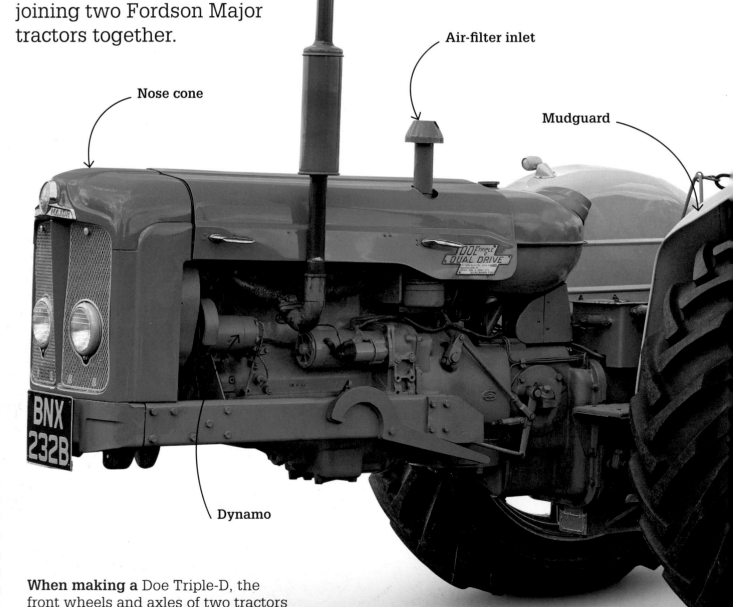

Nose cone

Air-filter inlet

Mudguard

BNX 232B

Dynamo

When making a Doe Triple-D, the front wheels and axles of two tractors are removed, and the tractors are joined together by a turntable, so that the tractor can bend.

As UK farms rapidly grew bigger in the 1950s, farmers needed more powerful tractors. By joining two tractors, the Doe Triple-D became a four-wheel-drive tractor with twice the power of most available tractors at the time.

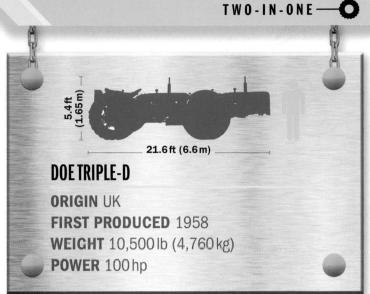

5.4 ft (1.65 m)

21.6 ft (6.6 m)

DOE TRIPLE-D

ORIGIN UK
FIRST PRODUCED 1958
WEIGHT 10,500 lb (4,760 kg)
POWER 100 hp

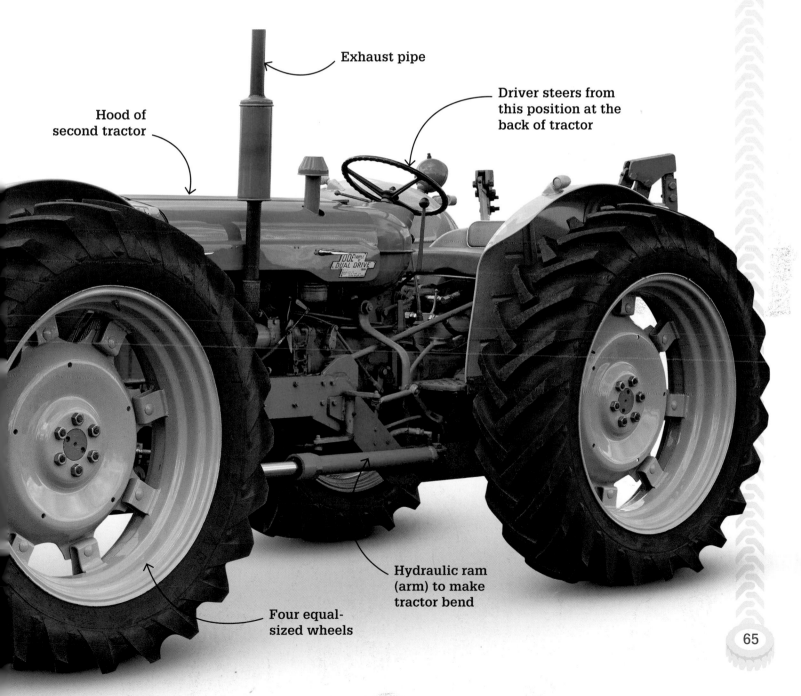

Exhaust pipe

Driver steers from this position at the back of tractor

Hood of second tractor

Hydraulic ram (arm) to make tractor bend

Four equal-sized wheels

EXTRA LARGE

Make way! Here come the true giants of the tractor world. These massive tractors were designed to pull extra-wide plows and cultivators over vast, tillable farmland, but their weight and width make most of them far too heavy and clumsy for working around delicate crops or in small spaces.

Large, equal-sized wheels

▲ FLEXIBLE TRACTOR

MASSEY FERGUSON 1200	USA 1972

This four-wheel-drive tractor is "articulated," meaning that it can bend in the middle. A tractor this big has to bend, otherwise it would need a huge amount of room to turn in a circle.

▼ EIGHT-WHEELER

VERSATILE BIG ROY	CANADA 1977

The Versatile company was famous for making large tractors, but it only ever built one "Big Roy." This 22-feet (6.7-meter) wide, 600-horsepower monster tractor now resides in a museum in Manitoba, Canada.

Big Roy weighs in at 28.6 tons (26 metric tons)!

▼ WORLD'S BIGGEST

BIG BUD 16V 747 | **USA 1978**

There was only one Big Bud 747 ever made. It became famous for being the world's biggest tractor, and its tires are 8 feet (2.4 meters) in diameter.

16-cylinder Detroit Diesel engine

Large radiator contains liquid to cool engine

◄ FOUR-TRACK DRIVE

CASE IH STEIGER QUADTRAC

USA 1996

Huge tractors can compact the soil, making it unproductive. This tractor has wide tracks to prevent that problem.

Triangular track frame

► HEAVY DUTY

KIROVETS K745

RUSSIA 2002

This vast articulated tractor is built in Russia by the Kirovsky Zavod company, which has been building powerful heavy-duty tractors since 1962.

Flight of steps to driver's cab

8-wheel drive

67

MONSTER TRACTOR

Ever since the 1950s tractors have been growing in size. Today's high-powered tractors can tow massive machinery with ease, allowing farmers to work large fields quickly and efficiently. The tractor's cab offers a comfortable seat, press-button controls, air-conditioning and even soundproofing, making life much easier for the driver.

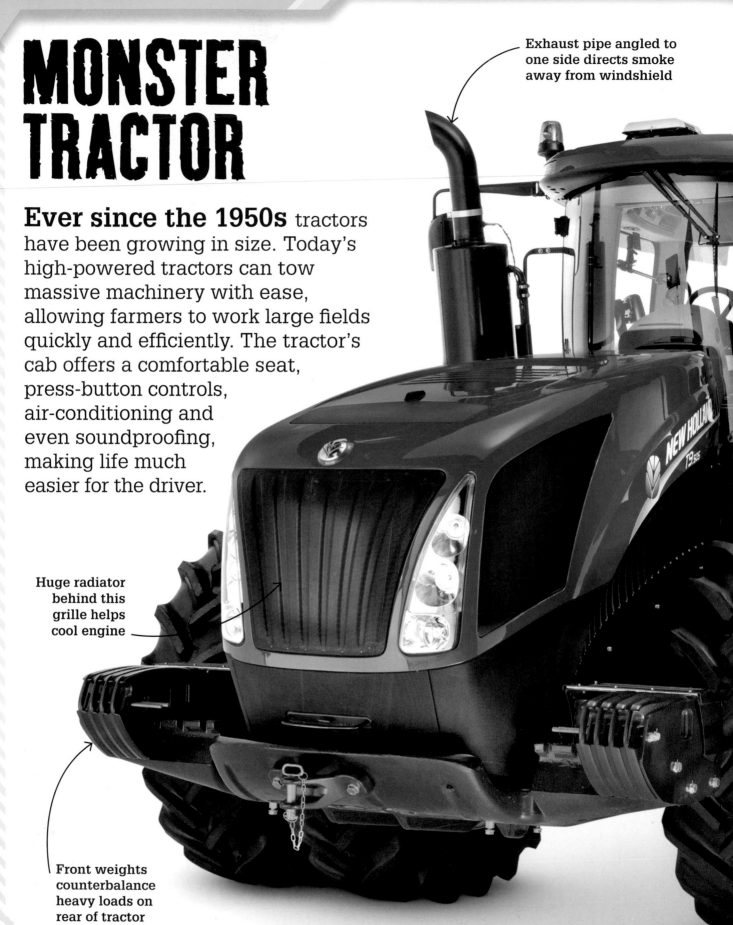

Exhaust pipe angled to one side directs smoke away from windshield

Huge radiator behind this grille helps cool engine

Front weights counterbalance heavy loads on rear of tractor

Antenna for picking up radio signals

Large mirrors provide good visibility

Extra wheels can be added to give better grip and even more pulling power. They also help to stop the tractor from sinking in soft ground.

12 ft (3.7 m)

24.7 ft (7.5 m)

NEW HOLLAND T9.505

ORIGIN USA
FIRST PRODUCED 2013
WEIGHT 49,500 lb (22,450 kg)
POWER 457 hp

"King Pin" holds together two parts of tractor

Some tractors are articulated, meaning that they are split into two and hinge in the middle. These tractors are extremely easy to steer and are able to turn around in a very small space.

** Farm gateways have had to be widened to make room for these giant tractors. **

A TIGHT SQUEEZE

A tractor from the 1940s would look like a tiny toy if parked next to a giant such as this John Deere 9400. There is, however, a limit to how large farm tractors can be. Most tractors have to travel on roads, and some of today's massive monsters already struggle to fit on narrow farm lanes.

ROW-CROP TRACTORS

These lightweight, nimble tractors were designed to work between rows of crops without damaging the plants. The driver has to position the tractor's narrow wheels carefully, so that they pass between or over the delicate growing plants.

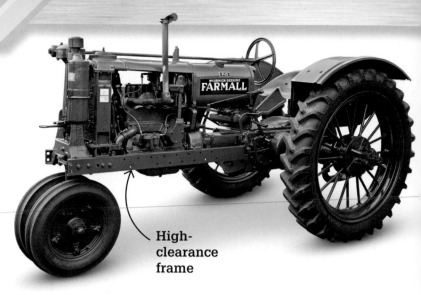

High-clearance frame

TURNING CIRCLE

By using the independent brakes to stop one rear wheel, the tricycle tractor can pivot around within its own length. The tractor can easily spin full circle, a feature that makes it excellent for maneuvering in confined spaces.

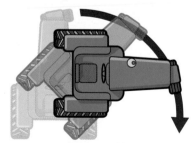

▶ SMALL BUT POWERFUL

JOHN DEERE B

USA **1935**

These popular little tractors have two-cylinder engines and a striking green-and-yellow body. Their unusual steering arm passes right over the top of the hood.

▲ TRICYCLE TRACTOR

FARMALL F-12

USA **1932**

These small, affordable tractors were hugely popular in the US. Early models were battleship gray, as seen here, but later examples were red.

▼ TRENDSETTER

OLIVER HART-PARR 70

USA **1935**

This tractor has a six-cylinder gas engine and an unusual streamlined shape, which was totally different from other tractors of the 1930s.

Closed-in engine compartment

Steering arm

Narrowly set front wheels

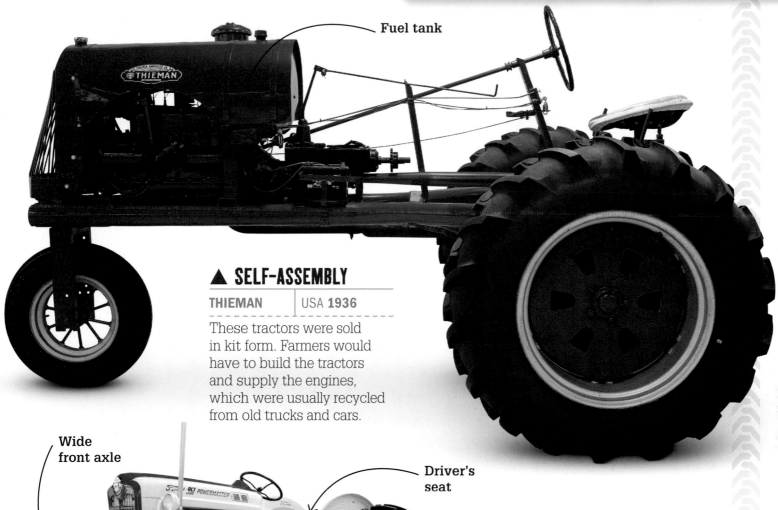

Fuel tank

▲ SELF-ASSEMBLY

THIEMAN | USA **1936**

These tractors were sold
in kit form. Farmers would
have to build the tractors
and supply the engines,
which were usually recycled
from old trucks and cars.

Wide
front axle

Driver's
seat

◄ MIGHTY WORKHORSE

FORD 951 HI-CROP

USA **1958**

This tractor has tall spindles
on the front axle to raise the
tractor high above the ground,
making it perfect for passing
over tall crops without
crushing them.

Exhaust
pipe

▶ POWERED STARTER

MASSEY-HARRIS 101 JUNIOR

USA **1939**

Early tractors were usually started
by turning a handle or a pulley, but
the 101 was one of the first tractors
to feature an electric starter.

A YEAR ON THE FARM

On most farms, the tractors work all year round. On a grain farm, tractors are first busy plowing and preparing the soil, sowing the seeds, and tending the crops—and then comes harvest time, the busiest season of the year.

❝ At harvest time tractors often work day and night. ❞

Newly sown seed is buried as drill moves along

Tines (prongs) break up and loosen soil

1. PLOWING AND CULTIVATING

A tractor will power and pull several different implements when preparing the soil for planting crops. Plows, cultivators, and harrows might be used to turn, loosen, and rake the soil.

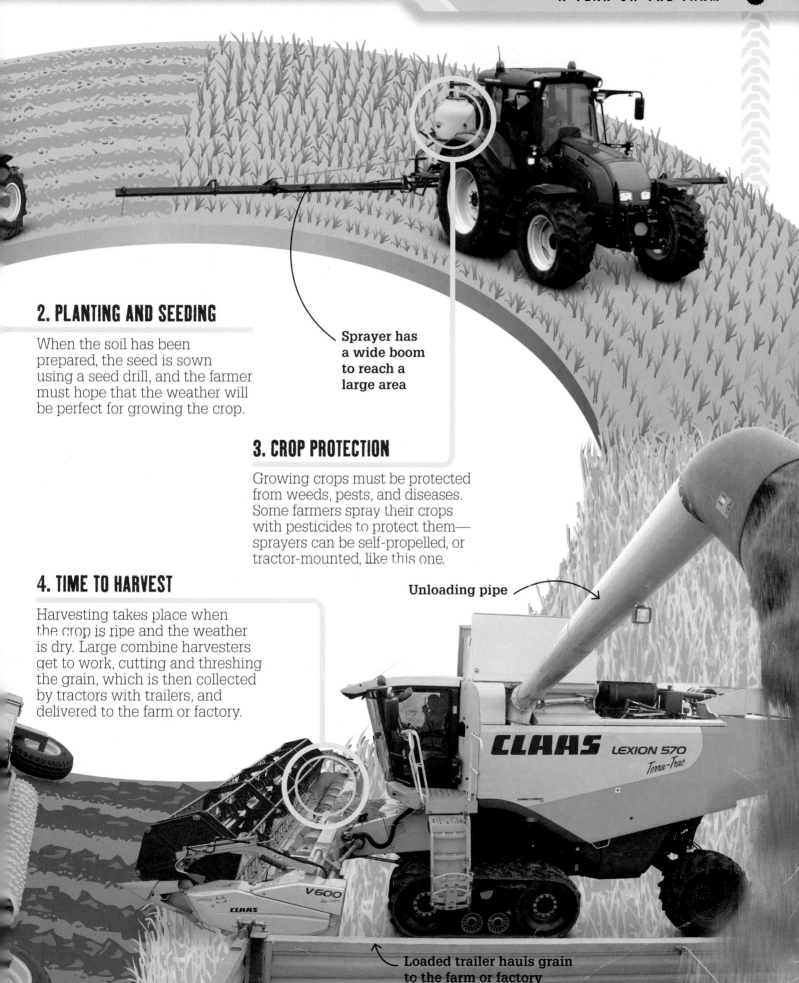

2. PLANTING AND SEEDING

When the soil has been prepared, the seed is sown using a seed drill, and the farmer must hope that the weather will be perfect for growing the crop.

Sprayer has a wide boom to reach a large area

3. CROP PROTECTION

Growing crops must be protected from weeds, pests, and diseases. Some farmers spray their crops with pesticides to protect them— sprayers can be self-propelled, or tractor-mounted, like this one.

Unloading pipe

4. TIME TO HARVEST

Harvesting takes place when the crop is ripe and the weather is dry. Large combine harvesters get to work, cutting and threshing the grain, which is then collected by tractors with trailers, and delivered to the farm or factory.

CLAAS LEXION 570 Terra-Trac

V600

Loaded trailer hauls grain to the farm or factory

EARTH-BUSTER

Huge modern plows are heavy farming tools pulled along by powerful tractors to break up the soil and turn it over. The blades bury weeds and loosen up the ground to create furrows ready for seeding or planting. Modern plows often have many blades.

In spring, the fields are plowed before the farmer can sow seed or plant crops.

Moldboards (cutting blades) turn soil

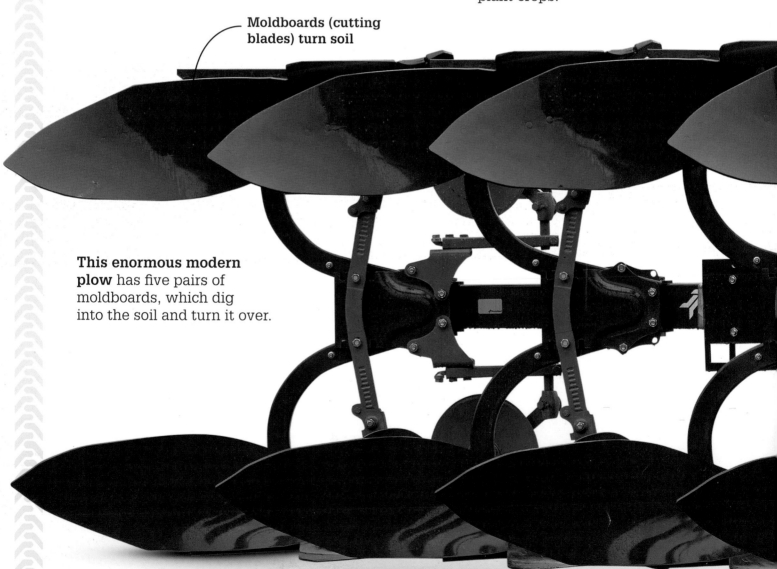

This enormous modern plow has five pairs of moldboards, which dig into the soil and turn it over.

REVERSIBLE PLOW

A double or reversible plow has opposing sets of blades that can be rotated. At the end of each row, the plow is turned over so that the other side can be used for the next row. Plows with a single set of blades can only plow in one direction, so a tractor would have to go all the way around the field to start a new furrow.

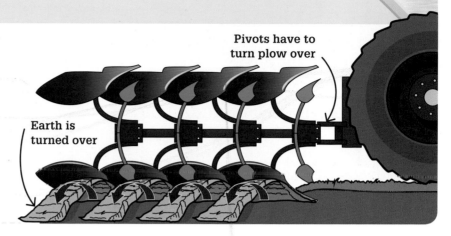

Pivots have to turn plow over

Earth is turned over

Plow is attached to back of tractor

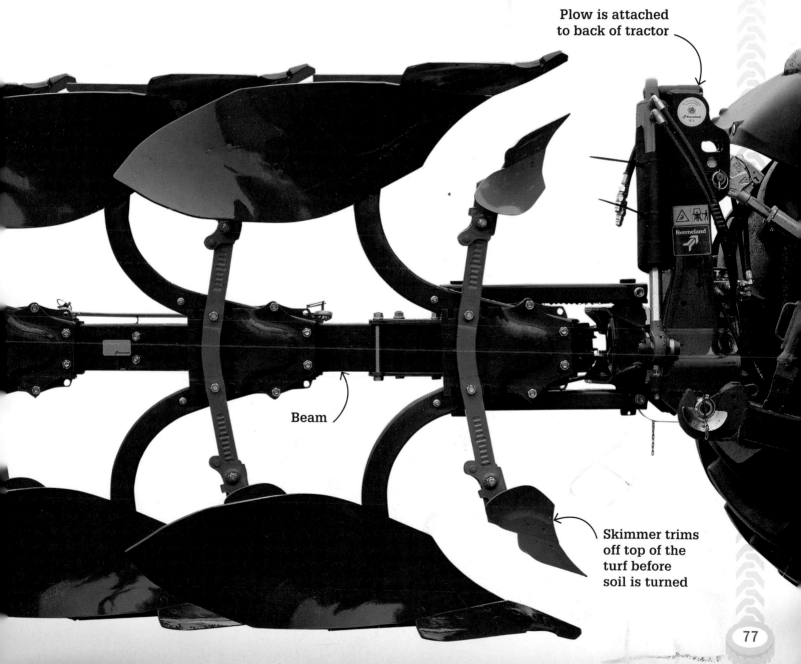

Beam

Skimmer trims off top of the turf before soil is turned

TURNING THE LAND

Even with the help of heavy-duty tractors, multiple-furrow plows, and hi-tech cultivators, farmers and tractor drivers still have to work very long hours. At busy times of the year, the tractor drivers switch on their lights at dusk, so they can continue plowing through the night.

SOWING SEEDS

Farmers use seeds to grow crops for food, medicines, clothing, and even fuel. These seeds must all be planted in the soil, and the seed drill can sow seeds far faster than any human can. Hand-powered seed drills were invented thousands of years ago in Mesopotamia (modern-day Iraq), and have since evolved into complex pieces of farm equipment.

Using a modern seed drill, the farmer is able to sow seeds over huge areas of land quickly and efficiently.

The seed drill didn't become popular worldwide until British inventor Jethro Tull perfected a horse-drawn drill in 1701. Tull's invention led to the development of modern farming, as well as many sophisticated implements such as this seed drill.

HOW SEEDS ARE PLANTED

As the drill moves along the ground, the coulters cut slots in the soil. The seeds travel from the hopper, down the pipes, and into these slots. The tines at the rear of the drill then rake the soil back over the seeded ground. Some drills may spread fertilizer at the same time.

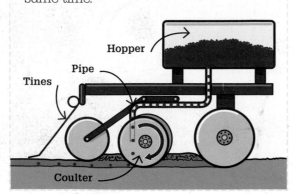

Hopper

Pipe

Tines

Coulter

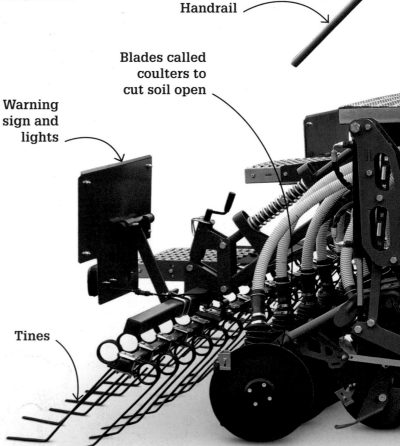

Handrail

Blades called coulters to cut soil open

Warning sign and lights

Tines

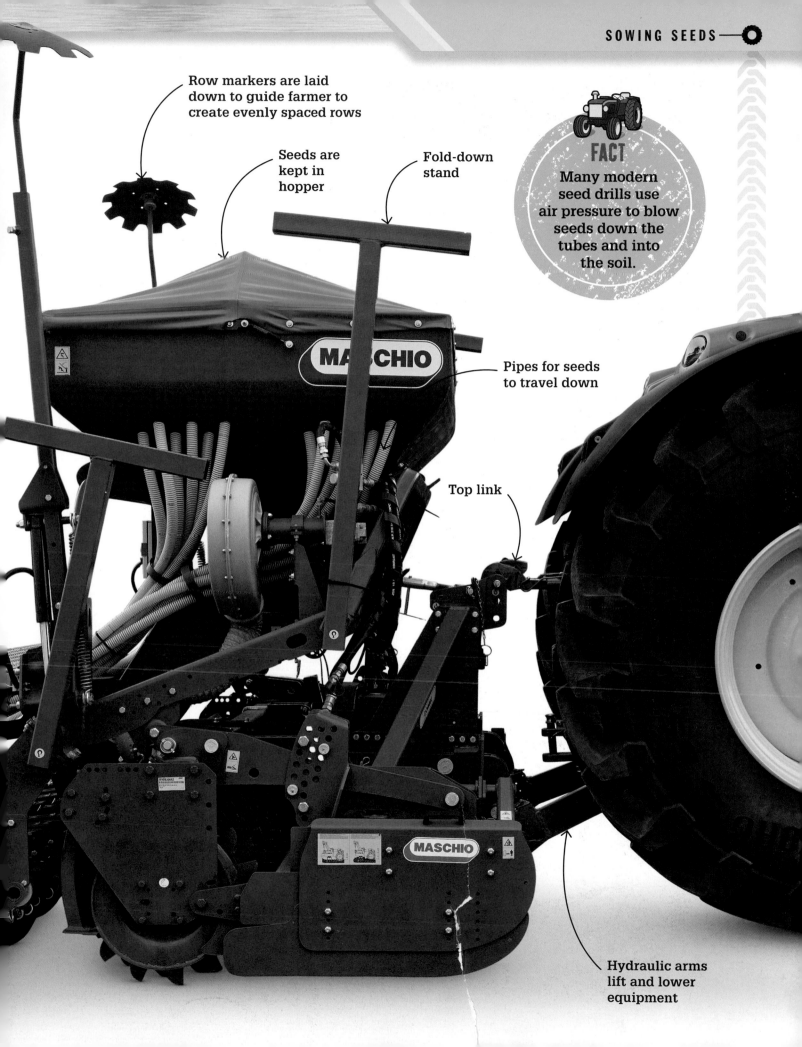

Row markers are laid down to guide farmer to create evenly spaced rows

Seeds are kept in hopper

Fold-down stand

FACT

Many modern seed drills use air pressure to blow seeds down the tubes and into the soil.

Pipes for seeds to travel down

Top link

MASCHIO

MASCHIO

Hydraulic arms lift and lower equipment

SPRAYING AND SPREADING

Healthy land means healthy crops. Plants must have nutrients to grow properly, and they must have some protection from pests, diseases, and weeds. Specialized implements have been designed to help farmers feed and protect their growing crops.

Flails are fitted inside cylindrical body

Fertilizer hopper (tank)

Fertilizer shoots out from here

▲ SPREADING FERTILIZER

AMAZONE PROFIS HYDRO | GERMANY

Chemical fertilizer comes in tiny pellets of nitrogen, phosphorous, and potassium, and is sprinkled evenly over the land by the spreader.

Large boom section is spread out for use

Huge hoses suck the slurry up into tank

Hydraulic pipes

Hitch to connect to tractor

▲ SLURRY SPRAYER

JOSKIN MODULO2 | BELGIUM

Slurry (animal waste) is pumped into this tanker, then sprayed out of the rear of the machine, onto the fields.

Stand (for when sprayer is not in use)

Muck gets flung from here

◀ FEEDING THE SOIL

ROTATING SPREADER	UK

Manure is seriously smelly but it is the most natural fertilizer. This "rota-spreader" uses a rotor equipped with flails to fling the muck sideways onto the fields.

Manure can be loaded using digger or loader

▶ MUCK SPREADER

TEAGLE TITAN 10	UK

This "rear discharge" manure spreader, made by British manufacturer Teagle, throws the muck out of the back.

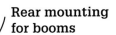

Power takeoff shaft powers spreader

Rear mounting for booms

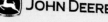

◀ CHEMICAL SPRAYER

JOHN DEERE M740i

USA

This implement sprays the growing crop with various chemicals that protect the plants from weeds, insects, and diseases.

SPRAYING CROPS

If a growing crop is destroyed by insects or disease, the farmer will lose a great deal of money. To prevent this from happening, farmers sometimes protect their crops by using tractors to spray pest and weed killers or herbicides.

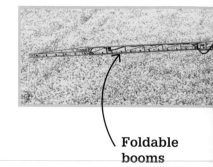

Foldable booms

Sometimes farmers need to kill off weeds that grow between plants, since these can dominate the valuable crop. The weed-killer sprays are called herbicides.

Large tank filled with herbicides

Central mounting for boom

Boom pivot point

The arms that reach out on each side of the sprayer are called "booms." The liquid travels down each boom and is sprayed over the crop. Long booms can spray over a very wide area.

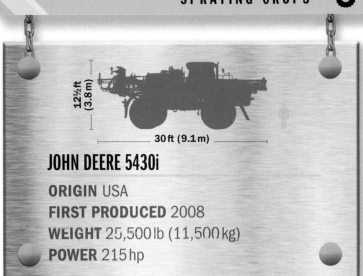

12½ ft (3.8 m)

30 ft (9.1 m)

JOHN DEERE 5430i

ORIGIN USA
FIRST PRODUCED 2008
WEIGHT 25,500 lb (11,500 kg)
POWER 215 hp

Protective cab

These booms can be stretched to an overall width of 118 ft (36 m).

Boom section folded up

Cab steps

Some small sprayers can be tractor-mounted, but specialized machines such as this self-propelled, high-clearance sprayer can save the farmer a lot of time. It can spray fields quickly, efficiently, and safely.

87

COLORFUL CROPS

Not all crops are for food. Large fields of lavender, grown for the perfume and cosmetic industry, are harvested by specially designed machines. A harvester cuts the plants into a dome shape and throws the flowers up into the trailer. This old John Deere tractor is the perfect width and height to fit over the rows of plants.

GRASSLAND FARMING

Grass is the main food for sheep, cattle, and horses. Grass grows quickly during the summer, so farmers cut it and store it for winter use. Silage is grass that is stored while still damp. Hay is grass that is dried and baled.

Front-mounted mower

▲ MOWING THE FIELD

MASSEY FERGUSON 146F | USA

Once the grass has grown long, it is ready to be cut to make hay or silage. This front-mounted mower cuts the grass neatly at ground level.

Rakes are folded up to travel on the road

Warning sign

▲ SPIN AND RAKE

MASSEY FERGUSON RK 3875 | USA

This wide machine unfolds when it is in the field. It lifts the cut hay and shapes it into neat rows, ready for the baler to pick it up.

FACT

Before machines, farmers made hay stacks by hand using pitchforks.

Rubber skirting prevents stones or sticks from flying out while mower is working

Front platform can be removed and replaced with different headers to suit a variety of crops

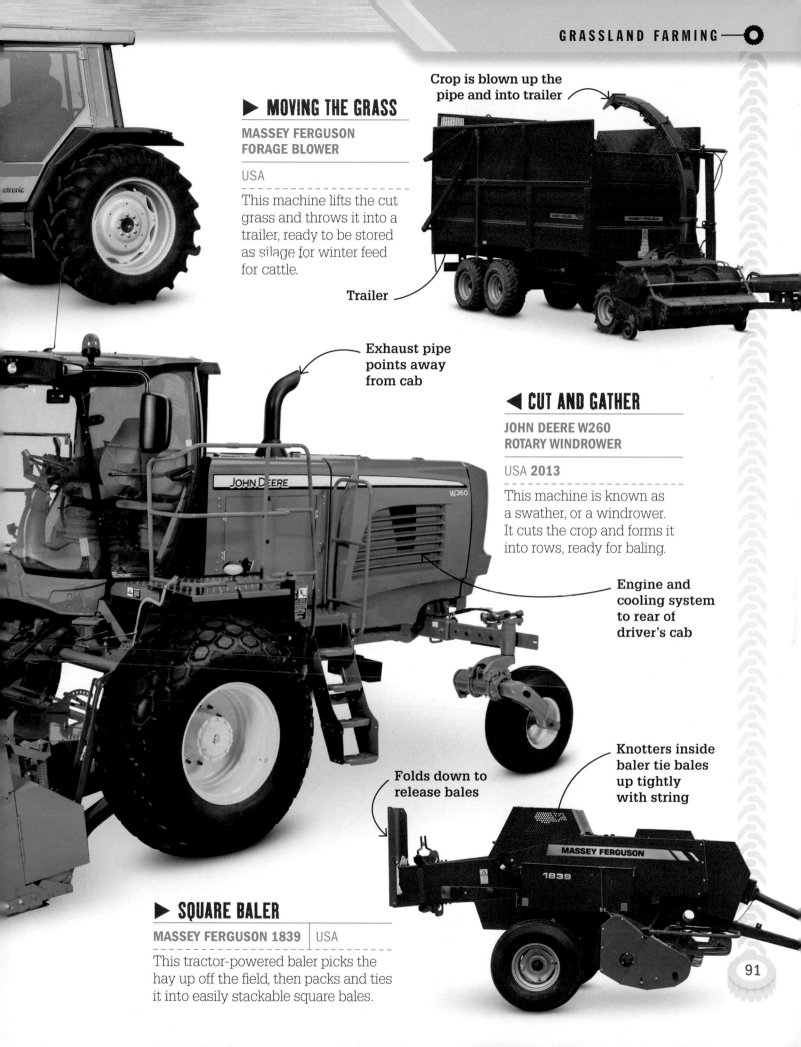

▶ MOVING THE GRASS

**MASSEY FERGUSON
FORAGE BLOWER**

USA

This machine lifts the cut grass and throws it into a trailer, ready to be stored as silage for winter feed for cattle.

Crop is blown up the pipe and into trailer

Trailer

Exhaust pipe points away from cab

◀ CUT AND GATHER

**JOHN DEERE W260
ROTARY WINDROWER**

USA 2013

This machine is known as a swather, or a windrower. It cuts the crop and forms it into rows, ready for baling.

Engine and cooling system to rear of driver's cab

Knotters inside baler tie bales up tightly with string

Folds down to release bales

▶ SQUARE BALER

MASSEY FERGUSON 1839 | USA

This tractor-powered baler picks the hay up off the field, then packs and ties it into easily stackable square bales.

91

BALING HAY

Hay was once stored in loose stacks, but today there are machines to pack the hay into shaped bales. These tightly packed bales take up less space than loose hay, and they can be stacked in large piles with a tractor and loader.

This round baler will tie the finished hay bale securely, either with string or with a net. Sometimes bales are wrapped in plastic so that they can be stored outside.

Completed bale drops out of tailgate

JOHN DEERE

MAKING BALES

The pickup reel and screws (augers) carry the hay up into the bale chamber. Wide belts or rollers wind the hay around, tightly compressing it into a cylindrical shape.

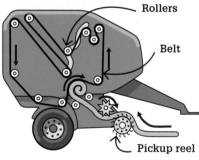

Rollers

Belt

Pickup reel

Step 1 The pickup reel lifts the hay into the baler.

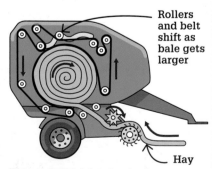

Rollers and belt shift as bale gets larger

Hay

Step 2 Inside the bale chamber, the hay is spun into a heavy, round bale.

Bale ejector

Once the bale reaches full size, it is tied tightly then deposited out of the tailgate of the baler. Baling on a slope has to be done carefully, so that the round bales don't roll away downhill!

Bale chamber

" Hay is simply dried grass. It can be fed to cattle, sheep, and horses during the winter months when grass is in short supply. "

960

Power takeoff shaft

Handle to wind down stand

Pickup reel

Hitch hooks baler to back of tractor

COMBINE HARVESTER

Farmers grow wheat to make the bread and breakfast cereals that we all enjoy. In the past, harvesting grain took a long time and many farm workers. Today's mighty combine harvesters do the job of several machines and can quickly and efficiently harvest vast grain fields.

Once the grain is cleaned, it passes into a storage tank. The grain is unloaded through a pipe straight into a nearby grain trailer.

Crops are cut at ground level and the augers drag the crop into the machine, where the edible grain is separated from the straw.

GPS receiver

Rearview mirror

Reel to draw crops toward cutter

Soundproof, dustproof cab

Cutter bar

The entire header can be removed, and for road transportation it is towed lengthwise on a trailer.

Augers

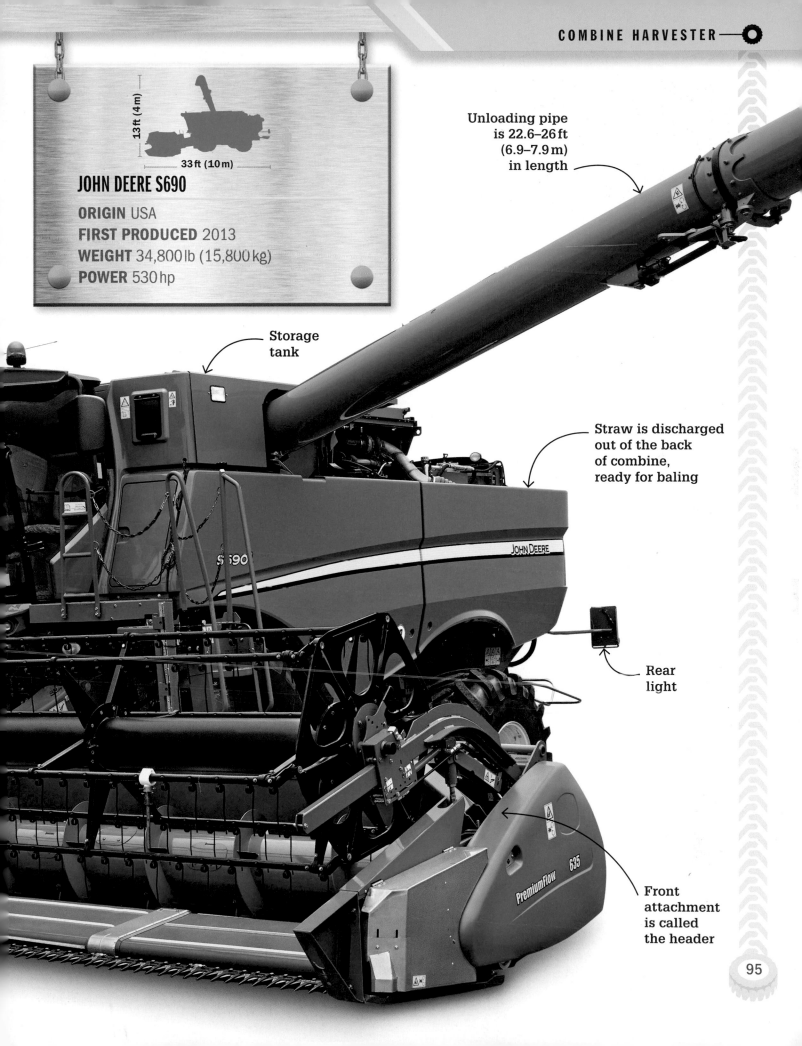

13 ft (4 m)

33 ft (10 m)

JOHN DEERE S690

ORIGIN USA

FIRST PRODUCED 2013

WEIGHT 34,800 lb (15,800 kg)

POWER 530 hp

Unloading pipe
is 22.6–26 ft
(6.9–7.9 m)
in length

Storage
tank

Straw is discharged
out of the back
of combine,
ready for baling

Rear
light

Front
attachment
is called
the header

PremiumFlow 635

JOHN DEERE

95

HARVESTING GRAIN

The mightiest machine on the grain farm is the combine harvester. A superwide header and a massive engine helps this huge beast harvest hundreds of tons of grain each day. This amazing piece of technology allows farmers to produce food on a much larger scale than ever before.

PUMPKIN PICKER

Not all tractors are mass-produced—some of them, such as this pumpkin harvester, are custom-built to suit the needs of certain farmers. Skilled agricultural engineers can use the engines, gearboxes, and axles of other tractors and different add-ons to build their own specialty tractor.

Powerful lights allow harvesting to continue into the night

Huge curved windshield gives driver an excellent view

FACT

This impressive harvester can process as many as three million pumpkins in just three weeks.

This tractor acts as a mobile packing and washing unit. It has "crawler gears," which allow it to creep along slowly across the field, keeping pace with the fruit pickers as they collect the ripe pumpkins.

Slatted elevator carries pumpkins up into holding tank

High sides prevent pumpkins from rolling off elevator

Pumpkins are picked and laid gently on to conveyor belt

" **Pumpkins are carved into jack-o'-lanterns at Halloween.** "

12 ft (3.6 m)

40 ft (12 m)

CUSTOM-BUILT PUMPKIN HARVESTER

ORIGIN UK
FIRST PRODUCED 2006
WEIGHT 5,300 lb (24,000 kg)
POWER 200 hp

Holding and cleaning tank

Water tank provides water for washing pumpkins

Workers stand at the rear and collect washed pumpkins from conveyor belt

Pumpkins are placed in crates ready to be lifted by another tractor and carried to the transport trucks

Wide tires prevent tractor from sinking in soft soil

SUGAR BEET HARVESTER

The large white roots of a plant called sugar beet *(Beta vulgaris)* are used to produce much of the sugar that so many people enjoy. Millions of tons of these roots are harvested each year by mighty machines designed especially for this task.

FACT

A video link inside the cab lets the driver see what is going on in each part of the machine.

Like a portable factory, the sugar beet harvester moves over the field, topping, lifting, sieving, and cleaning the precious sugar beet roots. Up to 22 tons (20 metric tons) of beet can be stored in the harvester's "bunker" before it must be emptied.

Orange warning lights

Powerful lights help driver work at night

Large, curved windshield gives a good view of machine's header

Defoliating unit cuts off leaves

Guide sensors

Rubber guard

Oppel wheels lift beets from the soil

13 ft (4 m)

41 ft (12.5 m)

GRIMME REXOR 620

ORIGIN Germany
FIRST PRODUCED 2012
WEIGHT 11,750 lb (25,900 kg)
POWER 490 hp

HOW IT WORKS

Sharp blades chop the leaves off the beets, and wheels (called oppel wheels) lift them up into the harvester. The beets roll and bounce through a series of turbines, slatted elevators, and conveyors, until the soil has fallen away. The cleaned beets are then ready to be unloaded into nearby trailers.

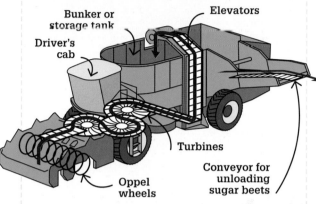

Bunker or storage tank

Elevators

Driver's cab

Turbines

Oppel wheels

Conveyor for unloading sugar beets

Auger spreads beets around in bunker

Slatted elevators carry beets into bunker

Hydraulic ram lifts and lowers unloader

Unloading conveyor

Cleaning turbine

Wide wheels for low ground pressure

This harvester can travel along roads at 25 mph (40 km/h), and although it's a huge machine, an articulated joint at the rear of the cab makes it easy to steer.

GRIMME

ORCHARDS AND VINEYARDS

Tractor manufacturers have been building narrow tractors, which fit between rows of trees and vines, for many years. But recently, more specialized machines have come onto the market—and some of these are barely recognizable as tractors.

Extra low cab to drive under trees

▲ SUPER SKINNY

FENDT 211V | GERMANY **2009**

Fendt makes these tractors in various widths. This model is extra narrow, and is used in vineyards.

Hopper (storage tank)

Cab

▲ OLIVE PICKER

NEW HOLLAND BRAUD 9090X | USA **2011**

This tractor passes over the olive bushes, shaking the plants until the olives fall off and are collected in the hopper.

▶ INCLINE SPECIALIST

MASSEY FERGUSON 3350C | USA **2001**

Steep slopes can be dangerous, but crawlers are more stable than wheeled tractors, making them ideal for hilly farmland.

Safety frame in case tractor rolls over

Narrow body

Large mirrors allow driver to see all around

Engine is opposite driver's cab

Frame to protect windshield from branches

▲ GRAPE HARVESTER

NEW HOLLAND BRAUD 9060L | USA **2013**

This bizarre-looking specialized machine is king of the vineyard. It straddles the rows of vines, collecting grapes for winemaking.

◄ LOW PROFILE

NEW HOLLAND T4 COOL CAB | USA **2014**

This little farm tractor is designed to pass under low branches. It is especially useful when harvesting nuts and apples.

SPECIALIZED TRACTORS

These four-wheeled

row-crop tractors are designed to squeeze between rows of growing plants and to pass easily over the tops of tall crops without flattening them. Raised "high-clearance" frames and super-skinny wheels are essential gear for these crop-field kings.

Hydraulically driven cutter head

6-cylinder engine

◀ GREEN MACHINE

OLIVER 1650

USA **1964**

The driver of this tractor can easily see all four wheels, and can carefully avoid driving over precious crops.

▶ TALL BOY

DAVID BROWN 850

UK **1960**

Early high-clearance tractors had no rollover protection and could be dangerously unstable. Modern ones are equipped with either a roll bar or a safety cab.

Adjustable backrest

Crop sprayer

Standard-sized front wheels on tall spindles

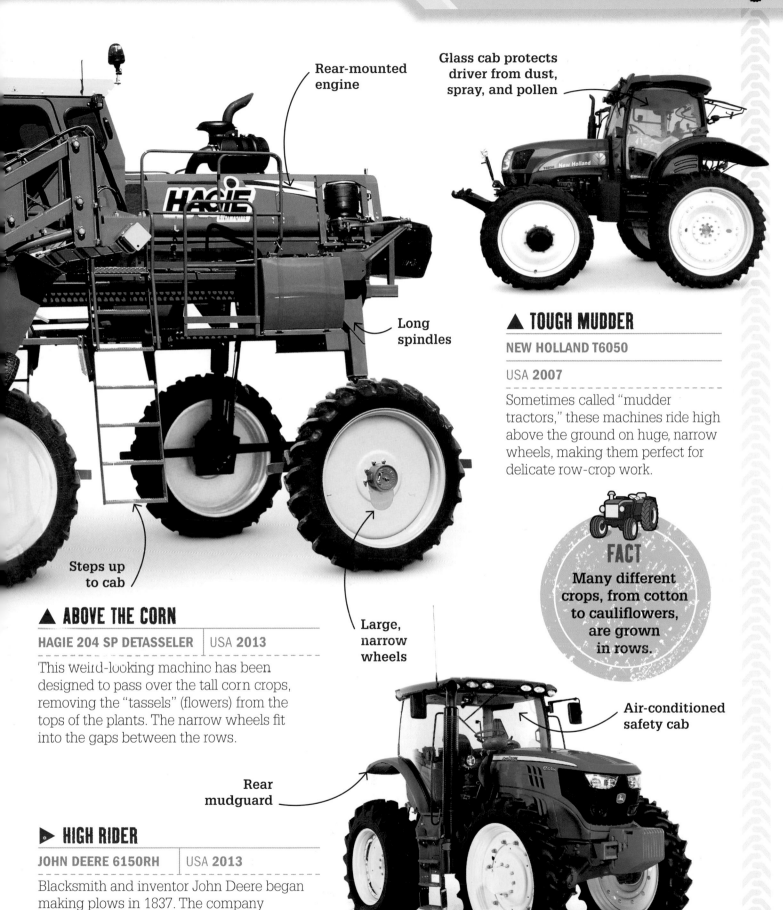

Rear-mounted engine

Glass cab protects driver from dust, spray, and pollen

Long spindles

Steps up to cab

Large, narrow wheels

▲ TOUGH MUDDER

NEW HOLLAND T6050

USA **2007**

Sometimes called "mudder tractors," these machines ride high above the ground on huge, narrow wheels, making them perfect for delicate row-crop work.

FACT

Many different crops, from cotton to cauliflowers, are grown in rows.

▲ ABOVE THE CORN

HAGIE 204 SP DETASSELER | USA **2013**

This weird-looking machine has been designed to pass over the tall corn crops, removing the "tassels" (flowers) from the tops of the plants. The narrow wheels fit into the gaps between the rows.

Air-conditioned safety cab

Rear mudguard

▶ HIGH RIDER

JOHN DEERE 6150RH | USA **2013**

Blacksmith and inventor John Deere began making plows in 1837. The company now produces a huge range of tractors and implements, including specialized machines, such as this high-clearance row-crop tractor.

POWER LIFT

Loaders are strong

lifting arms that can be fitted to tractors to make them more versatile around the farm. These arms can be equipped with different attachments, such as pallet or muck forks. Grabs and spikes can also be used; these allow the tractor to lift and stack bales of hay or silage (feed for livestock).

Large windows and glass doors for 360° vision

Mudguard

Distinctive gray Massey Ferguson rim color

A loader with a bucket is useful for lifting and loading grain, manure, fertilizer, and animal feed. It saves the farmer a huge amount of time and hard work.

Front tires have extra grip for 4-wheel drive

WORKING THE ARMS

The driver can control the modern loader from within the cab by using a joystick. Moving the joystick back and forth raises and lowers the loader arms, while moving the stick from side to side tips and crowds, or pivots, the loader bucket.

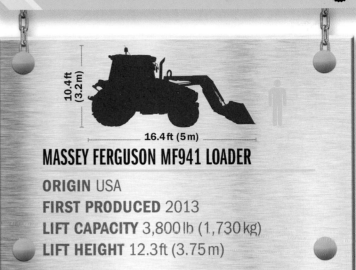

MASSEY FERGUSON MF941 LOADER

ORIGIN USA
FIRST PRODUCED 2013
LIFT CAPACITY 3,800 lb (1,730 kg)
LIFT HEIGHT 12.3 ft (3.75 m)

10.4 ft (3.2 m)
16.4 ft (5 m)

The entire loader can be removed, allowing the tractor to do everyday farmwork.

Loader bucket

Front loaders lift up high, allowing the driver to reach to the top of hay stacks, or to tip material into high-sided trailers.

Hydraulic rams help lift bucket

LOADERS AND HANDLERS

Gone are the days when tractors simply plowed fields and hauled trailers. Modern machines are now capable of grabbing, lifting, and carrying all kinds of materials. These loaders and handlers have amazing strength, and they make the farmer's work safer and easier.

Loader can be fitted with different types of buckets and forks

◀ BUCKET WITH GRABBER

MASSEY FERGUSON 8925 XTRA	USA 1998

This telescopic handler has an extending boom that allows it to reach up to 18 feet (5 meters) in height. The loader can lift weights up to 5,500 pounds (2,500 kilograms).

▶ MANURE FORK

MASSEY FERGUSON	UK

Farmers used to "muck out" their cattle by hand, using a pitchfork, but this tractor can clean out a large outbuilding with much less effort.

This tractor can lift manure and load it onto a trailer.

Hydraulic rams open and close grabber's jaws

Fork prongs grab and hold silage

◀ BALE GRABBER

NEW HOLLAND 740 TL	USA 2013

This tractor's grabber can lift and stack round bales carefully, without damaging the plastic wrap around the hay bales.

▼ ROUGH TERRAIN FORKLIFT

CATERPILLAR TH406 | USA **2010**

Useful in both agriculture and construction, this powerful tele-handler has a boom at the front that extends forward and lifts loads upward.

Pallet forks to lift loads

HYDRAULIC POWER

The tractor's engine powers a pump, which pushes hydraulic fluid down through pipes into a cylinder. As the pressurized fluid enters, it forces the piston out. The piston's movement lifts the loader arms.

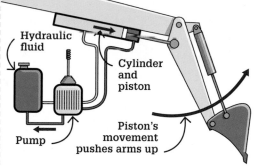

Hydraulic fluid

Cylinder and piston

Pump

Piston's movement pushes arms up

▶ SILAGE GRABBER

NEW HOLLAND 740 TL

USA **2013**

The loader on this tractor can grab, lift, and load manure or silage, saving the farmer hours of hard work.

NEW HOLLAND

740TL

TOWING TRAILERS

Trailers are essential for moving goods, including farm produce, materials, livestock, machinery, and animal food. Most farms own several different types of trailer, with each one designed for a specific task.

Hay ladder

▲ HAY RIDE

| BALE TRAILER | UK |

The front axle can swivel on this heavy-duty hay trailer, which enables it to follow the tractor around corners with ease.

▼ SILAGE SHIFTER

| RICHARD WESTERN SUFFOLK TRAILER | UK |

This silage trailer will be extremely busy at harvest time, carting the newly mown silage from the fields to the farmyard.

MASSEY FERGUSON 7619

RICHARD WESTERN

SF14HS

Twin axle

High-capacity tipping body

Train of
five trailers

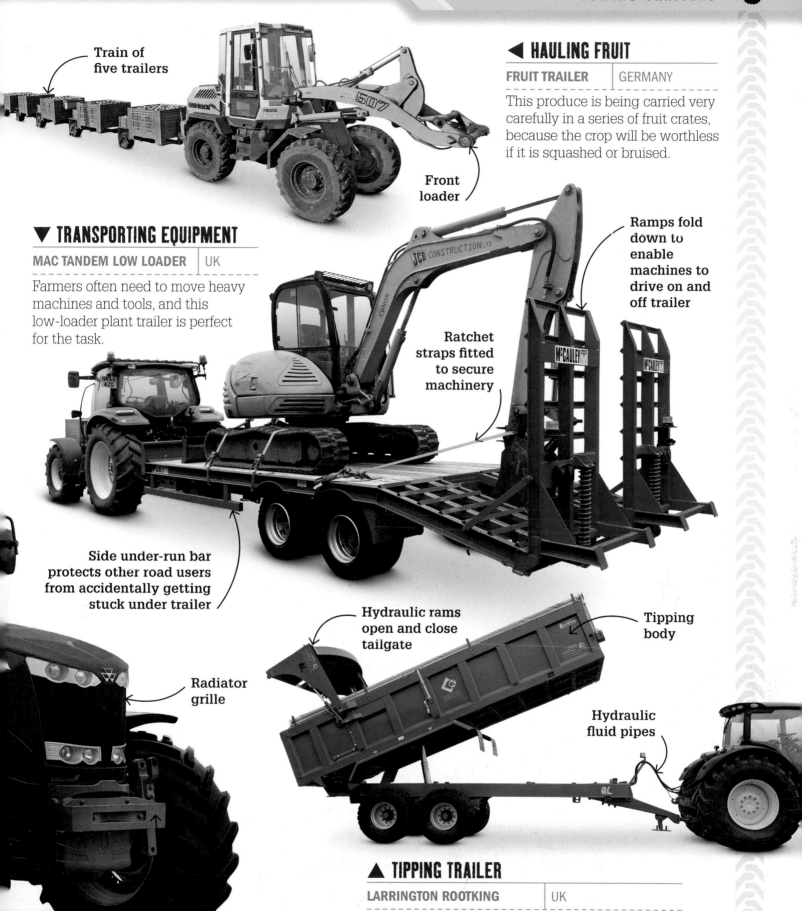

◀ HAULING FRUIT

FRUIT TRAILER | **GERMANY**

This produce is being carried very
carefully in a series of fruit crates,
because the crop will be worthless
if it is squashed or bruised.

Front
loader

Ramps fold
down to
enable
machines to
drive on and
off trailer

▼ TRANSPORTING EQUIPMENT

MAC TANDEM LOW LOADER | **UK**

Farmers often need to move heavy
machines and tools, and this
low-loader plant trailer is perfect
for the task.

Ratchet
straps fitted
to secure
machinery

Side under-run bar
protects other road users
from accidentally getting
stuck under trailer

Hydraulic rams
open and close
tailgate

Tipping
body

Radiator
grille

Hydraulic
fluid pipes

▲ TIPPING TRAILER

LARRINGTON ROOTKING | **UK**

This twin axle trailer is ideal for hauling heavy
root crops, such as potatoes and sugar beets. The
hydraulic rams lift and lower the tipping body.

Front
weight frame

BEYOND THE
FIELDS

AROUND THE YARD

These tiny tractors

are the gardener's best friend. They can be used for hauling tools and materials. The riding mower allows the gardener to mow large areas of lawn without breaking a sweat.

Cab without doors

▲ ALL-AROUNDER

JOHN DEERE GATOR

USA **1992**

For jobs around a large yard or property, this little utility vehicle can carry two people plus equipment and materials in the rear.

▶ BIG MOWER

JOHN DEERE 1565

USA **2002**

This professional version of a riding mower has a front-mounted mower deck, a cab that offers excellent visibility, and wide tires for grass.

Engine cover

Roll Over Protection System (ROPS)

Mower deck follows contours of the ground

▶ SPEEDY 4X4

MASSEY FERGUSON 1540

USA **2005**

This compact, three-cylinder diesel tractor is considered small by today's standards, but it is the same size as most of the British tractors of the 1940s and 50s.

MASSEY FERGUSON

1540

Driver's step

Operator's seat

▼ EASY RIDER

JOHN DEERE Z445

USA 2009

Mow your lawn from the comfort of your own chair. This easy-to-steer riding mower has a 27-horsepower engine.

EZtrak

Mower deck

Brodie knob (for steering with one hand)

◄ RIDING MOWER

MASSEY FERGUSON 21–25 GC

USA 2010

This might look just like a baby tractor, but it's a riding mower with a 25-horsepower engine.

Sun shade

Hydraulic rams move loader arms

MASSEY FERGUSON

► COMPACT POWER

NEW HOLLAND BOOMER 30	USA **2011**

Compact tractors are useful for big yards, small farms, and horse stables. They can be fitted with specially made, scaled-down implements.

BOOMER 30

NEW HOLL

Front bucket for shifting and lifting materials

115

TRACTORS AROUND TOWN

Power takeoff shaft powers mower

These busy urban tractors work tirelessly to maintain roads, parks, and grass shoulders in towns and cities. Mowers, flails, sweepers, and loaders are useful implements for the modern-day tractor about town.

▲ **ROADSIDE MOWER**

MASSEY FERGUSON 3065	USA 1992

This tractor is fitted with a front-mounted mower, which is ideal for cutting large roadside shoulders and rough areas of grass.

Unimogs can be fitted with different bodies for different jobs

▶ **ON THE RAILS**

UNIMOG U400	GERMANY 2000

Unimogs are multipurpose machines that can tow heavy loads and power various implements. They are used by municipalities in many countries.

Rotating scrubbing brushes

▲ **URBAN SPECIALIST**

HOLDER C270	
GERMANY 2010	

This versatile machine is shown here as a road sweeper, but it can also operate as a mobile water tank, snow-plow, or mower.

Wheels can be changed depending on type of work

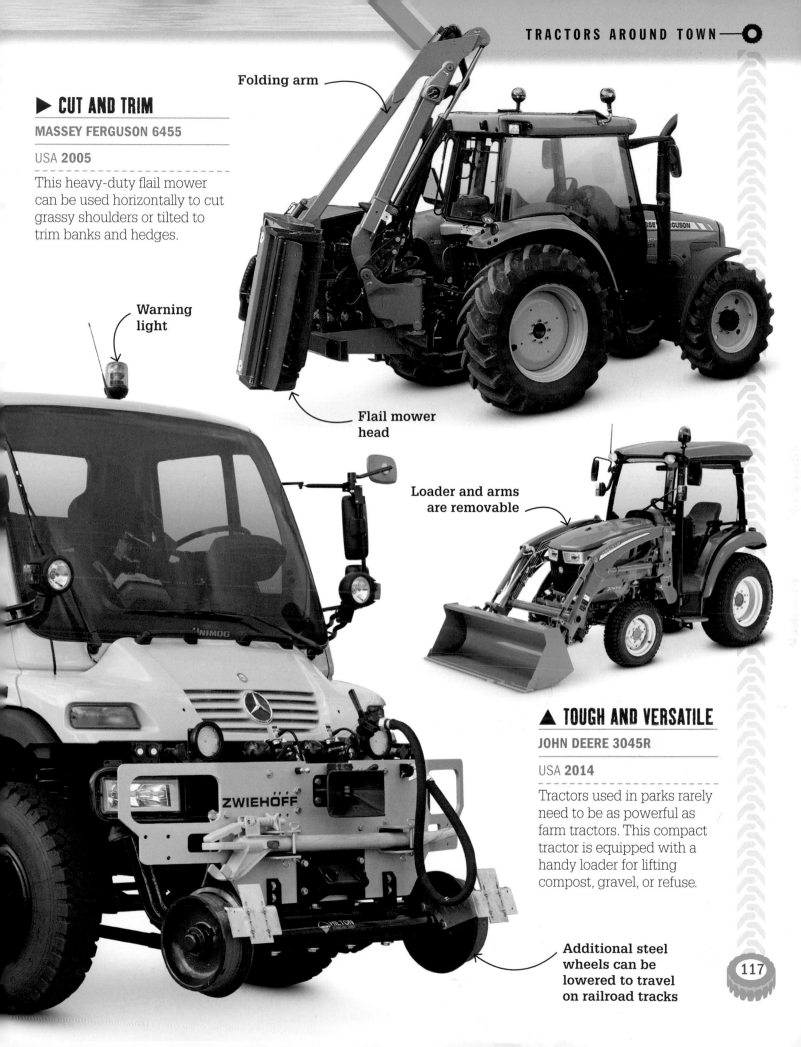

Folding arm

▶ CUT AND TRIM

MASSEY FERGUSON 6455

USA 2005

This heavy-duty flail mower can be used horizontally to cut grassy shoulders or tilted to trim banks and hedges.

Warning light

Flail mower head

Loader and arms are removable

▲ TOUGH AND VERSATILE

JOHN DEERE 3045R

USA 2014

Tractors used in parks rarely need to be as powerful as farm tractors. This compact tractor is equipped with a handy loader for lifting compost, gravel, or refuse.

Additional steel wheels can be lowered to travel on railroad tracks

PUSH OR PULL

Aircraft tugs, or "pushback tractors," are used to move airplanes around airports. This low-profile, heavyweight vehicle carries the nose wheel of the aircraft, and it pushes and pulls the plane carefully into position.

MILITARY TRACTORS

Some of the world's most advanced and exciting machines are owned by the military. Tractors, crawlers, and all-terrain haulers are very important to the armed forces. These machines help soldiers and their equipment cross safely over difficult and dangerous territory.

Chains beat hard on ground

High-clearance body for driving over obstacles

▲ HEAVY HAULER

BAZ-64022	RUSSIA **2007**

These Russian-built all-terrain transport tractors are capable of pulling huge weights, such as heavy artillery (guns) and missiles, over rough ground.

▲ CLEARING MINES

AARDVARK	UK **2008**

These amazing machines hunt for deadly land mines. They can clear mines from war zones, making the areas safe for people to inhabit once again.

EXPLODING MINES

Powerful spinning chains, known as flails, claw at the ground and pound it roughly, deliberately detonating any buried land mines. The mines explode, but the driver and the vehicle remain unharmed as the machine is heavily armored.

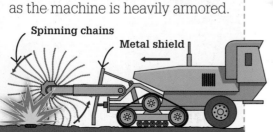

Spinning chains

Metal shield

Exhaust cap to prevent rain from entering pipe

Tiller wheel

▲ VETERAN TRACTOR

HOLT 75	USA **1913**

During World War I, thousands of Holt tractors were used for hauling heavy artillery. They were also designed for farming and road-building.

This haulage tractor is towing a trailer full of missiles.

Heavy-duty tires to cope with stony or muddy ground

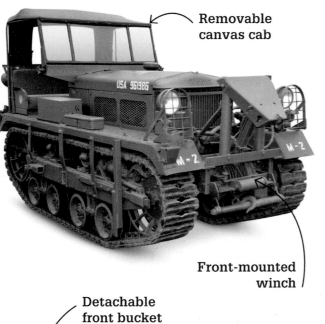

Removable canvas cab

Front-mounted winch

Detachable front bucket

◀ SPEEDY CRAWLER

CLETRAC M2 HIGH-SPEED TRACTOR

USA **1942**

This aircraft tug was used by the US military to tow aircraft. It is equipped with a winch and is capable of speeds of 22 mph (35 km/h).

▼ WAR DIGGER

JCB HMEE

UK **2008**

Unlike most diggers, this backhoe loader can travel at high speeds and tow heavy loads. It is also armored to keep the driver safe.

Rear digging bucket

121

MILITARY MIGHT

The BAE Terrier is a bombproof beast that works as a digger, a front loader, and a tank. The heavily armored shell protects the two crew members from explosions, and the front and side buckets can clear any obstacles that lie in its path.

FACT
The BAE Terrier can be equipped with machine guns and grenade launchers.

Lifting arm

Driver

This terrier carries a "trackway" for making a temporary road

Drive sprocket

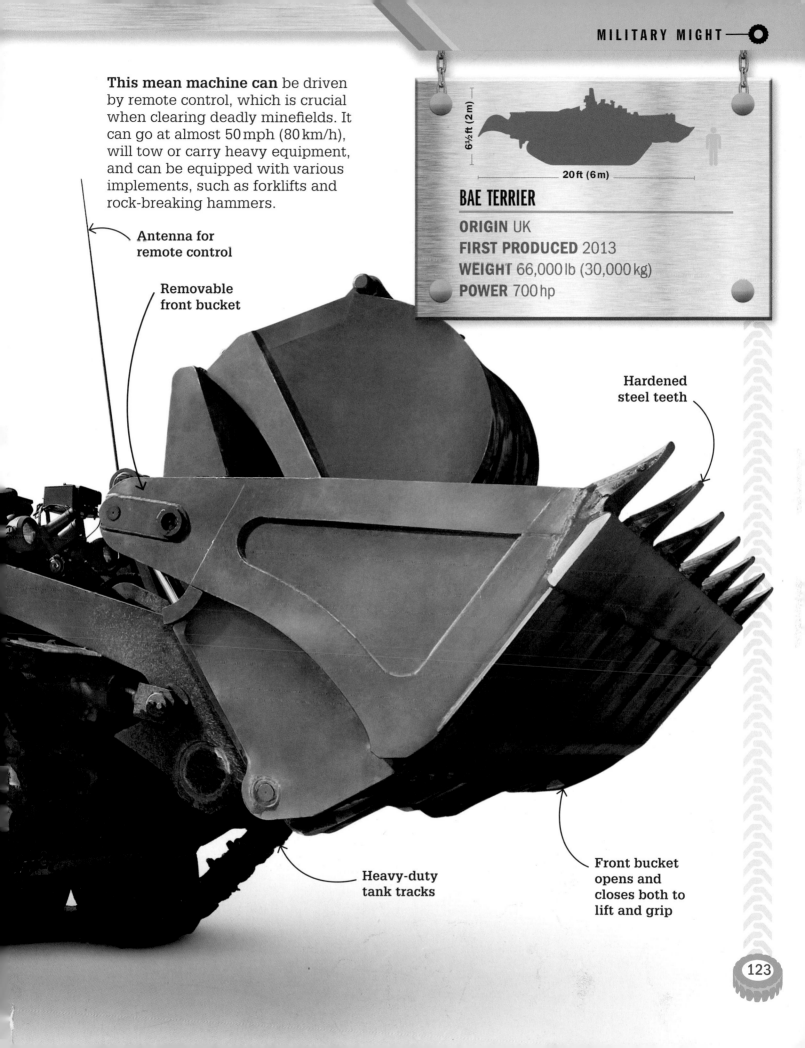

This mean machine can be driven by remote control, which is crucial when clearing deadly minefields. It can go at almost 50 mph (80 km/h), will tow or carry heavy equipment, and can be equipped with various implements, such as forklifts and rock-breaking hammers.

Antenna for remote control

Removable front bucket

6½ ft (2 m)

20 ft (6 m)

BAE TERRIER

ORIGIN UK
FIRST PRODUCED 2013
WEIGHT 66,000 lb (30,000 kg)
POWER 700 hp

Hardened steel teeth

Heavy-duty tank tracks

Front bucket opens and closes both to lift and grip

" The Talus MB-H works comfortably in up to 8-ft (2.5-m) deep water. **"**

A REAL LIFESAVER!

Specialty tractors such as this Talus MB-H are essential for hauling British Lifeboats in and out of the sea, even in rough conditions. The heavyweight 210-horsepower tractor was made in Wales, UK. It can be driven right into the sea—the cab and engine compartment are completely enclosed and watertight.

WINTER WONDERS

Tractors can be used to clear snow from our roads, to maintain ice roads and ski slopes, and as transportation or haulage vehicles in cold climates where cars and trucks cannot function.

Electrically heated windshield

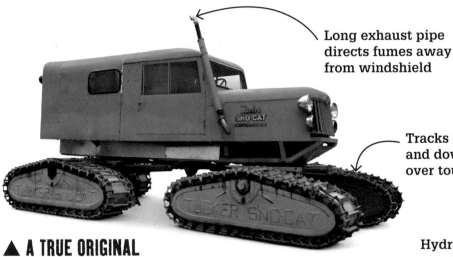

Long exhaust pipe directs fumes away from windshield

Tracks can tilt up and down to climb over tough terrain

Hydraulic pipes

▲ A TRUE ORIGINAL

TUCKER SNO-CAT

USA **1948**

With four independently sprung tracks and spacious cabs, these go-anywhere machines can carry passengers and equipment. They can even be equipped with front blades to clear snow.

Folding snow blade

FACT

Liquids in a tractor—oil, water, and fuel—need special additives to prevent frost damage.

▶ SKI GROOMER

PISTENBULLY PB260D

GERMANY **2007**

Extra-wide tracks and a highly maneuverable snow blade make this machine perfect for smoothing, grooming, and maintaining ski slopes and snow trails.

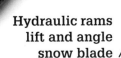

Hydraulic rams lift and angle snow blade

▶ BLOWING SNOW

KAHLBACHER KFS 950/2600

AUSTRIA 1995

Driven by the tractor's power takeoff shaft, this handy snow blower helps to keep our roads open by sucking up snowdrifts and blasting them away.

Pivoting spout to direct snow away

Augers (screws) to lift and shift snow

PB 260 D

▼ POWDER PUSHER

VALTRA T152 WITH SNOW PLOW

FINLAND 2011

Front blades, snow plows, or V-plows can be fitted onto most tractors, but it takes a powerful machine such as this Valtra to handle these large implements.

Superwide tracks spread the weight

Curved blade helps push snow to sides of road

THE COLDEST JOURNEY

Antarctica is the most hostile place on Earth. During the harsh winters there are vast ice fields, sheer crevasses, temperatures as low as −130°F (−70°C), and almost constant darkness. These super-tough Caterpillar D6N tractors were modified to cope with the demands of "The Coldest Journey"—an amazing tractor-powered expedition to cross the South Pole in winter.

Two Cat D6Ns worked together on this extreme expedition. Between them, these mighty machines hauled the team's living accommodation, supplies, and equipment across the icy wasteland.

" **A radar on the crevasse arms tells the driver exactly how thick the ice is.** "

Crevasse arms help prevent the vehicle from falling into deep holes and to lift itself out of difficulty.

SOLD & SERVICED BY FINNING

Huge blade to clear snow and obstacles

The crawlers have to cross crevasses in the ice. When this crawler got stuck, the second machine had to winch it out.

Wide tracks prevent vehicle from sinking

These tracks have large, castellated cleats (with blades shaped like castle walls), which penetrate the ice and provide grip. For climbing glaciers, spikes can be added to provide even stronger grip.

The modified tractors have a complex central heating system—this keeps the driver warm and also prevents the machine's working parts from freezing solid.

129

TRACTORS AMONG THE TREES

Forestry tractors are super-tough machines. They work hard on rough, uneven ground, scrambling over fallen branches and tree stumps. Enormous strength is required for these tractors to safely lift and haul heavy loads of timber.

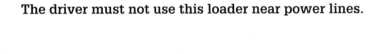

The driver must not use this loader near power lines.

▼ MIGHTY FORWARDER

PONSSE ELEPHANT | FINLAND **2011**

This forwarder can haul 20 tons (18 metric tons) of lumber, travel at 12 mph (19 km/h), and can work on rough terrain and snow.

Steel guard protects engine from knocks and bumps

Log bunks hold lumber in place

Safety frame protects tractor and driver from falling timber

◄ CABIN FOR THE WOODS

STEYR 4130 | AUSTRIA **2013**

Modern Steyr tractors are fuel-efficient, economical, and produce fewer harmful gases. This model has a protective cage for forestry work.

Special lumber trailer

Front blade clears obstacles and creates a path

Strong grapple claw

▲ GRAPPLE SKIDDER

JOHN DEERE 648H	USA **2008**

This powerful skidder has a high-clearance frame and a massive hydraulic grab that can lift and carry several trees at once.

▶ FULLY LOADED

VALTRA T162	FINLAND **2011**

A heavy-duty tractor, Valtra T162 is fitted with a "reverse drive" system, which allows the operator to drive it facing either way.

Hydraulic loader with extending boom

◀ TIMBER TRAILER

VALTRA N123	FINLAND **2014**

This multipurpose tractor is ideal for forestry work. The rear snow chains allow it to operate in all weather conditions.

Heavy-duty tires for rough terrain

131

TIMBER!

This logging tractor

acts like a ferocious forest beast, grabbing whole trees and cutting them off at the base. It is powerful enough to grab and fell more than one tree at a time. The mighty engine and huge wheels help it to climb over stumps and push through undergrowth with ease.

Hidden away between these mighty yellow jaws is a powerful saw, which slices easily through tough tree trunks. The machine then carries the lumber to a nearby stack or trailer.

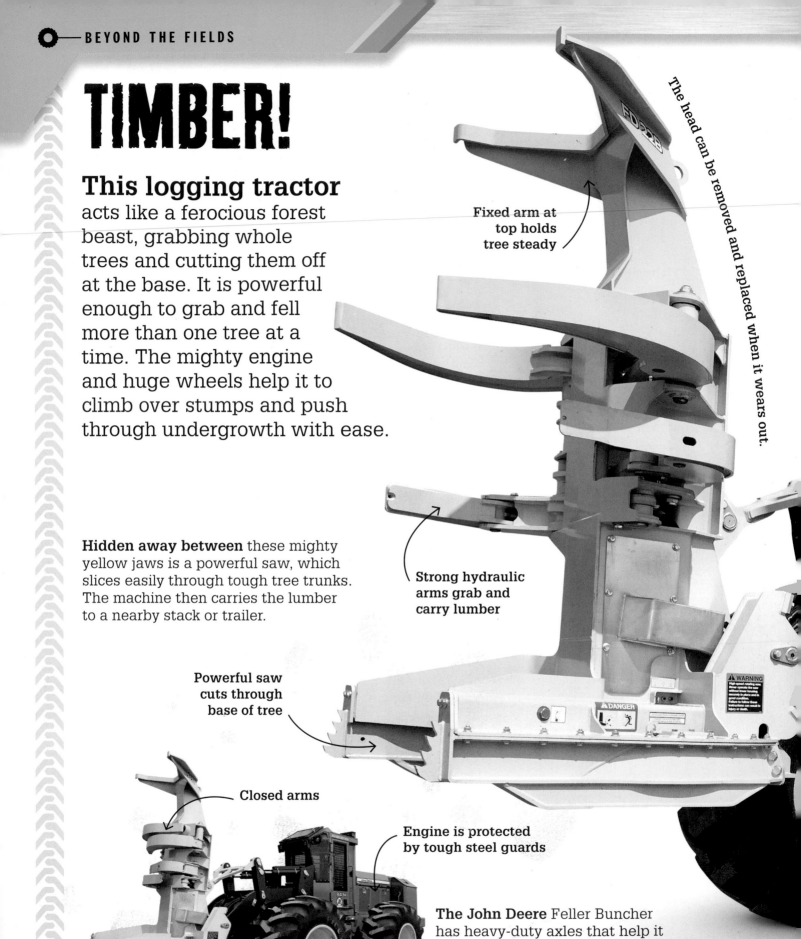

Fixed arm at top holds tree steady

The head can be removed and replaced when it wears out.

Strong hydraulic arms grab and carry lumber

Powerful saw cuts through base of tree

Closed arms

Engine is protected by tough steel guards

The John Deere Feller Buncher has heavy-duty axles that help it to work on rough, steep ground. The removable head bunches trees together and then fells them, which is why it is called a feller buncher.

This feller buncher can perform the work of several people with saws, and it makes tree felling much safer because the operator is housed in a protected cab.

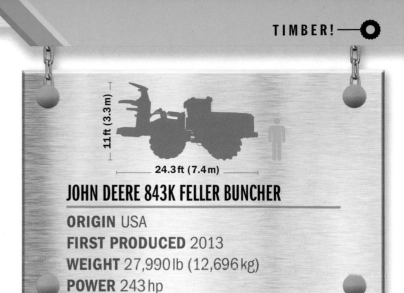

11 ft (3.3 m)

24.3 ft (7.4 m)

JOHN DEERE 843K FELLER BUNCHER

ORIGIN USA
FIRST PRODUCED 2013
WEIGHT 27,990 lb (12,696 kg)
POWER 243 hp

Air-conditioned cab has computer monitors, joysticks, and a radio

FACT

From huge tractors to tiny garden mowers, John Deere machines are easily spotted by their green and yellow colors.

KEEP BACK 300 FT / 90 M

JOHN DEERE

843K

Extra wide tires help to support this heavy machine on wet or uneven ground

MAJOR MOVERS

Tractors are excellent at multitasking—they can pull and power all types of tools. But some machines such as this grader have been created to do one job really well. This self-propelled grader can level (smooth out) large areas of land.

FACT
Some graders have a second blade mounted onto the front of the machine.

The superheavy frame helps to press the blade down on the ground.

Working light

672GP

Heavy-duty tires with industrial tread pattern

134

This machine uses its huge underslung blade to create a smooth surface on rough, uneven ground. Graders often prepare and maintain roads and construction sites, and can level areas where other machines have been working.

Hydraulic rams to lift, lower, and tilt grader blade

Driver's door

11 ft (3.4 m)

29 ft (8.9 m)

JOHN DEERE 672 GP

ORIGIN USA
FIRST PRODUCED 2013
WEIGHT 44,000 lb (20,000 kg)
POWER 240 hp

Soundproof cab

Engine bay

Adjustable grader blade to level soil

Clawlike ripper tine for breaking up compacted surfaces

135

EARTHMOVERS

These heavy-duty vehicles have been designed to work in the construction (building) industry, and they each have a specific job to do. Whether it is leveling ground, shifting materials, or laying pipes, there is a specialized machine available for every task.

▶ COMPACTOR

HAMM HD | **GERMANY 2009**

Designed to smooth out surfaces, this articulated tandem roller weighs in at almost 14 tons (12.7 metric tons) and is a real heavyweight.

Heavy-duty, smooth steel roller

Some scrapers have to be moved along by bulldozers.

▲ MOTOR SCRAPER

CATERPILLAR 615C

USA 2001

The scraper blade cuts into the ground, and conveyors carry the top layer of soil up into the hopper. When the hopper is full, it can be emptied at a convenient site.

Scraper blade

Hydraulic arm raises and lowers hopper

Wire ropes lift and lower boom

FACT

Some of the heaviest tractors in the world are used in the mining industry.

Winching equipment for lifting and hauling

◀ SIDE BOOM CRAWLER

CATERPILLAR 583T | **USA 2006**

This colossal crawler is part tractor, part crane. It has a tall boom on one side and is ideal for laying pipelines in deep trenches.

Roll Over
Protection
System
(ROPS)

Pegs to
crush and
compact
surface

HAMM

HD⁺140

WIRTGEN GROUP

Articulated joint
allows machine to
bend in middle

▲ SHEEPSFOOT ROLLER

SAKAI SV400 | JAPAN **2008**

This articulated compactor
has rubber rear tires and
a "sheepsfoot" or "padfoot"
roller drum with large pegs.

Safety frame
prevents injury
to driver

▶ DIRT DOZER

JOHN DEERE 650K XLT | USA **2012**

This tracked bulldozer is perfect for
road-building. It can move huge mounds
of soil and gravel using its large blade.

Vibrating
rollers help to
compact soil

650K
XLT

Bulldozer
blade

BIG AND BRIGHT

A huge variety of tracked and wheeled machines can be seen busy at work on today's construction sites. Dumpers, bulldozers, crawlers, and diggers are referred to as "plant." Yellow is the color of choice for these hardworking machines, simply because it is highly visible on potentially dangerous work sites.

HEAVY EQUIPMENT

Hardworking construction vehicles have evolved from basic tractors into specialized machines, designed to perform specific tasks on today's busy construction sites. Earthmoving vehicles need to be strong and durable because they have to dig, lift, and carry immense loads of soil, tarmac, and gravel.

This bendy heavyweight can get around sharp corners

▲ DUMP TRUCK

TEREX 2566B	USA **1992**

Heavy-duty articulated dump trucks can carry more weight than most tractors and trailers, and have become hugely popular in the road-building, construction, and quarrying industries.

Large bucket with teeth

◀ FRONT LOADER

CASE 621B	USA **1993**

This giant scoop on wheels is the expert when it comes to lifting and shifting huge loads of loose material.

Exhaust pipe

▶ BACKHOE LOADER

JCB 3CX	UK **2009**

With its front loader, rear arm, and wide range of available buckets, it's no wonder that the "digger" is a popular construction vehicle.

Roll Over
Protection
System
(ROPS)

◀ MINI DUMPER

BENFORD 4000 | UK **1994**

Small dumpers have been popular for decades on construction sites—they are more nimble than big dump trucks.

▶ SKID-STEER LOADER

NEW HOLLAND L225 | USA **2013**

The skid-steer is a low, compact machine that is extremely stable for its size. It is perfect for lifting and loading goods in confined spaces.

Tough industrial tires

Soundproof safety cab

The digger's arms are controlled by powerful hydraulic rams.

Bucket for digging holes and trenches

INDEX

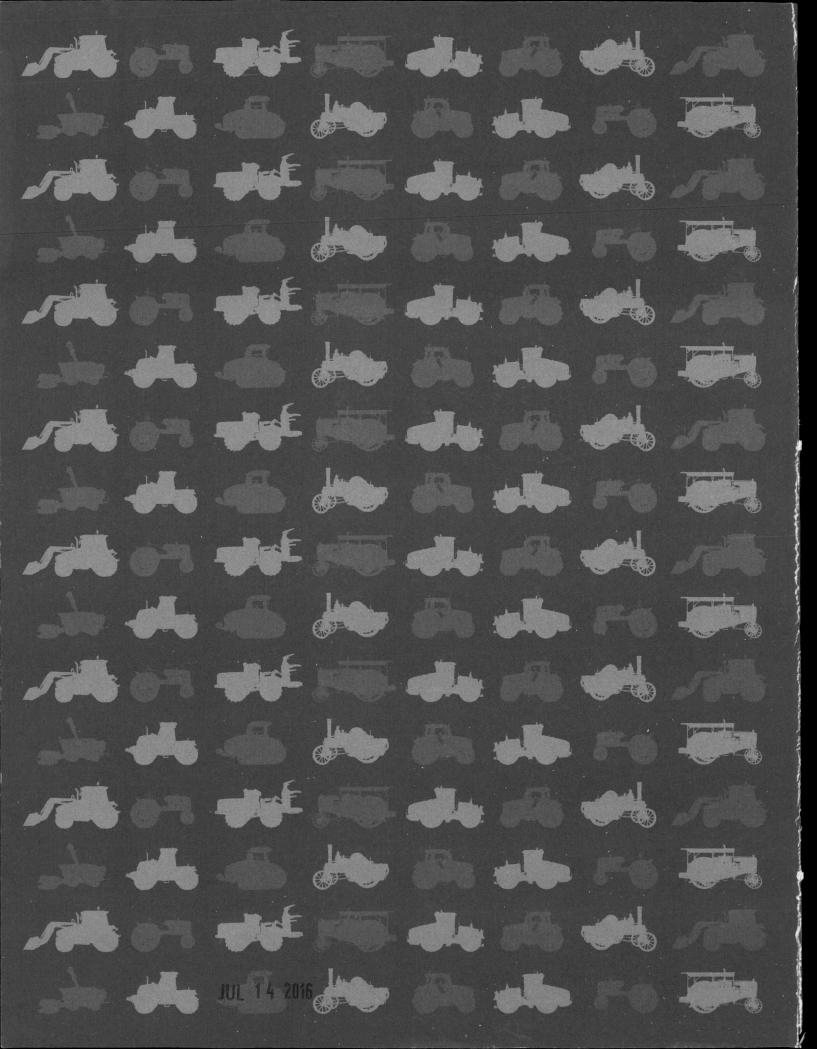